The Book of
GARDEN
GAMES

The Book of
GARDEN
GAMES

A COMPENDIUM OF OUTDOOR
PURSUITS THROUGH THE AGES

J. A. Wines

MICHAEL O'MARA BOOKS LIMITED

First published in Great Britain in 2003 by
Michael O'Mara Books Limited
9 Lion Yard, Tremadoc Road
London SW4 7NQ

A CIP catalogue record for this book is available
from the British Library

ISBN 1-84317-047-7

1 3 5 7 9 10 8 6 4 2

Designed and typeset by Martin Bristow

Printed and bound in Finland by WS Bookwell, Juva

CONTENTS

To my family, with thanks for your support
in the writing of this book,
and also to my sporting editor.

INTRODUCTION

THE British have always been a great nation of games players and our history is rich with the many traditional pastimes that were indulged in, come high day or holiday – from those played by the aristocracy and churchmen, to those enjoyed by common folk.

However, tracing the history of an individual game is not an easy task, as few are well documented. As we reach for the rules inside our new croquet set or tin of jacks, we might spare the thought that, at one time, much of the population would have been illiterate, so that game rules were passed on by active play and imitation, rather than through the written word. Naturally, different individuals or regions often felt the need to introduce their own interpretation of rules, and, in spite of attempts to standardize modern sport, there are still regional differences in the rules of many games – even those with national and international governing bodies.

In general, most of the games we play today are thought to have their origins in antiquity. Artefacts in ancient tombs, ancient drawings, and similar clues, lead us to believe that our ancestors played games akin to our own. Unfortunately, we cannot prove exactly which games they were playing; a set of ancient clay balls could indicate that our ancestors liked marbles, for example, or equally that they were playing solitaire.

Even the game immortalized by Sir Francis Drake at Plymouth Hoe is hotly contested, with pétanque historians, for example, asserting that the game played was not bowls. In many instances, it is only possible to speculate about the truth of these histories.

Our ancestors had less time to play games than we do today, but they made the most of it. In medieval times each holy day was associated with a sporting tradition, for example. Throughout the centuries kings, courts and churchmen regarded such occasions warily. For, while they wanted the population to be content, and for hot-blooded young men in particular to be able to let off steam from time to time, they were less tolerant of large and rowdy gatherings, betting on the outcome of games, and absences from church and archery practice – skill with the bow being integral to military success. Games also became linked to public houses, and many thus acquired somewhat unsavoury reputations.

At various times, bans were imposed on games, but it was not always possible to enforce these, so that, in spite of the threat of fines, people continued to indulge in the pastimes they enjoyed. As kings and church leaders themselves enjoyed sporting privileges, there was no rule by way of example. Henry VIII, by all accounts a very good games player, ran up large losses betting on the games he played, while Charles I was known to be excessive in his gaming pursuits.

The Puritans did their best to ban all sports and games that were played for pleasure. Again this was not particularly easy

to enforce, and although some games did cease to be played for a time, most were re-established after the Restoration.

In the late nineteenth century, there was a loss of interest in garden games due to the increasing popularity of team games such as rugby, cricket and football, which all encouraged spectating rather than participation. Additionally, there was more emphasis on 'manly' games, with the effect that croquet, bowls, archery, and even tennis acquired the reputation for being soft games. Of course anyone on the receiving end of a serve reaching a speed of more than 100 mph (161 kph), would hardly use the word 'soft' to describe the modern game. With the turn of the century, even popular garden games such as tennis and badminton had reached new levels of play, and were taken much more seriously, and today are regarded as professional and commercial sports.

Sadly, in current times, few of us regularly play the traditional games that were once commonplace. Often, while we might find suitable recreation in our own gardens, we head elsewhere for our entertainment, and many of our sporting pursuits are associated with fitness and weight-loss rather than fun. We probably visit the local gym or pool, or go jogging, before we ever think to get out our rounders bats or badminton rackets, for example. Increasingly, we 'play' alone, and our 'games' are much less social than they used to be, and often electronic rather physical.

The biggest recent threat to traditional game playing has been the advent of television and the computer game, both of which have driven people indoors. Although television has greatly increased the following of some games, it has also encouraged the overuse of the armchair and the remote control. Many of us who could participate in sporting activity, are now more content to watch others play.

If an excuse is needed to rediscover the game-playing potential of our gardens and how to have fun in the open air, it is hoped that this book might provide it. It is intended for sports and games lovers of all descriptions, even armchair enthusiasts, but it is to be hoped that people will be inspired to play the games written about here, as well as to read about them.

With this intention, the basic rules of each game, and the equipment necessary for play, are outlined, although an expert wishing to peruse these in great detail will need to look else-where. It should be noted that even today rules sometimes vary according to individual interpretation or regional play. Also, while the rules of some games have changed little since they were first set down, others may be updated frequently.

Most of the games in this book are intended for play by adults, and in none of them is an adult too old to play – even in hopscotch on the patio, or hide-and-seek in the shrubbery. Many can be played by families, and others require the cajoling of friends and neighbours.

Whether one prefers a simple pastime or a more challenging game requiring skill and finesse, be it the crack of croquet balls or the trajectory of the shuttlecock, this book is a perfect manual for games-loving and sporting enthusiasts.

Garden games do seem to be making a comeback. Although they are not included in this book, it is interesting to mention here that games of giant chess, giant stacking towers, giant lawn darts, and giant snakes and ladders have all found their way into retail outlets as garden games. Also, with every approach of summer, many shop shelves become crammed with boules and croquet sets, skittles, quoits, tennis rackets, swingball and badminton sets, and even bows and arrows. These are available as the more expensive traditional variety – as the famous Jacques brand – and also as cheaper sets. It would seem all is well with the British garden game, after all.

ARCHERY

THERE are probably not many of us who regularly wander out into our gardens, bow and arrow in hand. However, at one time in Britain, every male over a certain age was expected by law to practise shooting at targets, and in the nineteenth century archery was a popular sport in the grounds of the landed gentry.

In a sporting book of the 1940s, archery was described as: 'a most adaptable sport: 20 or 30 yards (18.3 or 27.4 metres) in a garden for short-range target shooting or 500 odd yards (457 metres) over fields for flight shooting are equally enjoyed by the bowman. Moreover shooting by himself gives the archer the opportunity to concentrate on improving his style and beating his previous scores, while shooting in competition with others adds to the pleasure of meeting good friends, without the novice in any way spoiling the game for the expert.'

The book goes on to recommend a good bow, six or more straight arrows, a bracer to shield the arm (from string burn) and a leather tab to protect the fingers, and – importantly – to remind would-be bowmen that arrows can be lethal, and that the utmost care in shooting them must always be observed.

Archery involves the use of a bow to shoot arrows at a target consisting of ten multi-coloured concentric rings. Each of the circles has a different point value, with those at the centre of the target having the highest; the innermost circle, or bull's-eye, usually has a target score of ten, while the outermost circle is worth just one point. Naturally enough, no points are awarded for a shot that misses the target.

For a fun game in the garden, one can buy a basic archery kit, comprising a target board, bow and a selection of arrows, the safest types being rubber-tipped or blunt-pointed, if children are likely to be playing too.

Today, target shooting is the most popular form of the sport, but other types of archery are also enjoyed such as field (shooting over a course, where one moves on to the next target – it actually has similarities to golf), flight (competing for who can shoot the furthest – the world record for the footbow is over a mile), clout (a rarer form, in which arrows are shot high into the air and should fall on a target laid flat on the ground), and 3-D archery (shooting at life-size replicas of various wildlife). One can even participate in ski-archery.

The bow and arrow was invented as far back as 25,000 years ago, and has been ranked in importance with the discovery of speech and the ability to make fire. Its use was widespread in the ancient world, and it allowed for significant advances in hunting and warfare, and thus for improvements in diet, clothing and safety. As a weapon, its accuracy ensured the best chance of hitting a distant target, until the much later invention of firearms.

Ancient bows varied in design. Some were short, others long; some were powerful, others weak; some suited hunters on foot and others those on horseback. Some were used for killing large prey, and some to kill fish. The weaker bows were sometimes used in conjunction with poison arrows. Interestingly, the word 'toxic' derives from the Greek word 'toxix', from 'toxicon', meaning 'poison arrow'. Followers of archery came to be known as 'toxophilites', a name that derives from the Greek word 'toxon', meaning bow.

In 3,500 BC, the Egyptians were using bows as tall as themselves. Almost 2,000 years later, the Assyrians developed the shorter recurve bow, which bent backwards, thus making it more powerful and easy to use. In the modern sport, arrows fired from a recurve bow can travel in excess of 150 mph (241 kph), and 225 mph (362 kph) in the case of compound arrows. The Parthians of Central Asia were famous for being able to shoot backwards from a galloping horse – hence the expression, to deliver a Parthian shot. In 1,200 BC, the Hittites developed the skill of shooting from moving chariots, and around 500 AD, the Romans began to draw the arrow to the face rather than from the chest, giving the shot more accuracy.

Arrows also varied, with arrowheads first being made of burnt wood, then stone or bone, and then metal. Egyptian arrowheads made of bronze date back to 3,500 BC. Initially, the bow and arrow were used for hunting and protection rather than for sport, but in Chinese history, nobles at court during the Chou dynasty of 1027–256 BC attended archery tournaments that were accompanied by music and entertainment.

From the reign of William the Conqueror, the longbow was England's principal weapon of national defence until the 1500s, being inexpensive, mobile, and accurate over a range of up to 250 yards (229 metres). At Crécy, in 1346, the new longbows showered arrows on the French, and honour on the English, and the English emerged triumphant again from the battlefields of Agincourt and Poitiers. Legend has it that the two-finger insult originated with the English archers at

Agincourt, the French having threatened to cut off their fingers, so that they would not be able to pull a bow. Thus, at the end of the battle, the English stuck their fingers up to prove their victory.

However, Englishmen were not allowed to rest on their laurels. The longbow took great strength to pull and years of practice to master, and successive governments did not forget this. All men and boys over a certain age were expected to practise regularly. In 1361, Edward III decreed that they must 'use bows and arrows or pellets or bolts and shall practice the art of shooting', and a further decree of 1363 required all Englishmen to practise archery on Sundays and holidays: 'Everyone in the shire, on festival days when he has a holiday, shall learn and exercise himself in the art of archery.' The authorities took a dim view when the populace showed itself more willing to spend their holidays indulging in other pastimes, and, as a consequence, most other sports and games were banned at one time or another.

Archery practice involved shooting over long distances for military training, but it would appear that rules, as well as bows, were bent – people finding it more enjoyable to shoot at closer range targets. However, archery was practised throughout the country and in all areas of society. In fifteenth-century Scotland, all males over twelve years of age were expected to spend time at the butts, and it was

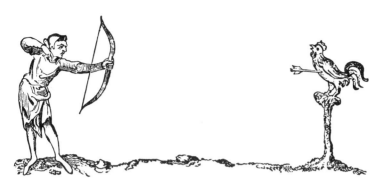

considered a civic duty to maintain local archery grounds. Unsurprisingly, many families took their names from archery, such as Archer, Arrowsmith, Bowman, Bownocker, Bowyer, Butts, Fletcher, Stringer, and Yeoman.

A popular archery sport practised with longbows was popinjay shooting, or *tir á la perche*, where birds were tethered on perches placed at different heights and shot at. The highest (which could be very high) was the king bird, or *coq*, with smaller birds at medium heights and the smallest on the bottom perches. Tradition has it that in the ancient Olympic games, the targets were tethered doves. The oldest recorded archery event in the British Isles is of this kind, and was first recorded in Scotland in 1483. The 'Papingo' shoot at Kilwinning, Ayrshire, is still held today and involves shooting down a wooden bird suspended from a pole at the top of the abbey tower.

Henry VIII possessed a breech-loading gun, but he preferred to sport with the bow and arrow. In 1510, it was said of him: 'His Grace shotte as stronge and as greate a lengthe as anie of his garde', and, according to G. A. Hansard, the king not only carried a longbow of the finest Venetian yew but, 'right well did Henry on that day maintain the reputation of his countrymen. He repeatedly shot into the centre of the white, though the marks were erected at the extraordinary distance of twelve-score yards apart.' Meanwhile a French contemporary said, 'They went to practise archery with the King of England, who is a marvellous good archer . . .' Henry VIII was patron of the Fraternity of St George, a company of archers that was formed in 1538, from which the Honourable Artillery Company also emerged in 1585.

In 1545, Roger Ascham, published the first book on archery written in English: *Toxophilus*. Although he was a Cambridge scholar, he acknowledged in the dedication that he had written his book 'in the English tongue, for Englishman' and that he had not employed his scholarly training in Latin or Greek so that as many people as possible could 'pleasure or profit' from the sport. Henry VIII engaged him to tutor his daughter Elizabeth.

By 1600, three kinds of archery were practised in England. 'Butt shooting' involved aiming at targets mounted on butts over ranges of 100–140 yards (91–128 metres). In 'clout shooting', arrows were shot at a canvas target, which was flat on the ground and had a wooden peg at the centre. 'Roving', meanwhile, emerged from hunting. (This later became the modern sport of field archery.) The Finsbury Archers had a roving course in Finsbury Fields, near London, in 1658.

The invention of gunpowder and use of firearms eventually overtook archery. In the defeat of the Spanish Armada in 1588, 10,000 English troops were equipped with firearms, while the Spanish were armed with bows and arrows. The rest is history, as they say, or at least it was for English archers in the matter of waging war. With no pressure upon the people to keep practising archery, interest in the bow and arrow saw a sharp decline. However, it was around this time that the sport of archery began to take off.

Sir Ashton Lever, a Lancashire baronet, is said to be the inventor of modern target archery. In 1781, he founded the Toxophilite Society, which made the sport fashionable with the gentry and which enjoyed the patronage of the Prince of Wales (later George IV). The Prince fixed the shooting lengths at 100 yards (91 metres), 80 yards (73 metres) and 60 yards (55 metres), and the values of the target rings as 9, 7, 5, 3, 1.

Archery meetings became great social events, with balls and theatricals taking place after the archers left the field. Meanwhile, parading in elegant shooting costumes was as important as the shooting itself, especially as ladies liked to spectate. Not many clubs included women as participants, although the Royal British Bowmen, founded in 1787, did so.

In 1793, *Sporting Magazine* listed twenty of 'the principal societies or companies of archers', which often had rather quaint names such as the Sherwood Foresters, the Bowmen of Chevy Chase, the Woodmen of Arden and the Robin Hood Bowmen and many of which had aristocratic patrons. Rival societies began to hold matches, and the beginnings of national contests were in place by the end of the eighteenth century. A national contest was not easy to initiate, however. War with the French severely disrupted the sport, and although efforts were made to introduce national meetings, interest was slow to take off. In 1843, for example, a silver cup was shot for at the Hull Zoological Garden, but although the meeting was 'open to all England', eleven out of the fourteen contestants were from Hull and the others from North Yorkshire. It was not until 1844 that a proper national contest was planned with the result that eighteen different societies in England and Scotland participated in the first Grand National Archery Meeting, held in York. From then on, the event was held annually at venues throughout the country, although since 1924 it has been held in Oxford.

In 1861, it was decided that archery needed a permanent governing body and the Grand National Archery Society was duly established, presiding over national contests and rules. It is still the governing body for target archery today, as well as field and flight archery.

By the early years of Queen Victoria's reign archery had become an established sporting exercise for ladies – in fact the Queen herself participated, and was patron of the Royal British Bowmen. In her *Lady Companion*, published in 1845, Miss Loudon writes: 'Archery is a favourite amusement with ladies in the country, as few exercises display an elegant form to more advantage. The first thing that is to be done is to choose a suitable piece of ground; and as most old houses have a piece of ground which was used as a bowling green, I have no doubt yours has one which will be quite suitable for the purpose. The ground having been chosen, the next thing is to set up the targets, and the next to provide proper bows and arrows, bracers, and shooting gloves . . .'

Showing oneself to advantage was important, as many young women were more interested in cupid's bows and the

field of husband-hunting than they were in shooting at targets. With the cream of society in attendance, archery meetings were excellent occasions for such pursuits.

From the 1850s onwards, archery had again suffered competition from firearms in the form of rifle shooting, and in the 1870s lawn tennis also raised a challenge to its popularity. Golf, cricket and rugby were also rival interests. However, the real threat to archery was urbanization as new building often swallowed up suitable grounds. Archery reached its peak in 1881 with some 130 clubs, after which there was a marked decline to about fifty in 1889.

Archery was represented in the Olympic Games in 1900 at the Paris Olympiad with shooting at 30 and 50 yards (27 and 46 metres) and popinjay shooting. At the 1908 British Olympics Lottie Dod (who had already won the women's lawn tennis championship at Wimbledon, aged fifteen, and then another four times after that) won the silver medal, and her brother Willy won the gold in the men's division. The gold and silver medals in the women's division were also won by British archers. Archery featured again in 1904, 1908, and 1920, but owing to the confusion which grew out of there not being any international rules, it was removed from the Olympic programme.

A desire to standardize the diffuse rules led to the formation of the International Archery Federation in 1931, which is still the governing body for the sport. In the same year the inaugural World Championships were held, and by 1972 archery was reinstated to the Olympics. Today the International Archery Federation has over one hundred member nations throughout the world.

BATTLEDORE
AND
SHUTTLECOCK

THE ancient game of battledore and shuttlecock must have been enjoyed by a great many people over the centuries, being a fun pastime that almost anyone above a few years of age could play. The game involves two or more players keeping a feathered object (the shuttlecock) in the air, by hitting it alternately with a bat or racket (the battledore). It

is a co-operative rather than a competitive diversion, the challenge of the game being the number of hits scored mutually before the shuttlecock falls to the ground. In 1830, the Somerset family, who obviously had very good hand-eye coordination, and excellent counting skills, recorded 2,117 hits.

The game developed in ancient Greece around two thousand years ago, and from there it spread to China, Japan, India and Siam. In medieval England it was documented as a recreation for peasants, and, by the late sixteenth century, it was looked upon as a children's pastime. However, in the seventeenth century it seems to have become popular once more with adults. In the 1660s, writer Edward Chamberlayne listed 'shuttle-cock' as a common divertissement among 'citizens and peasants', and it was also being played by the upper classes in many European countries. Numerous nineteenth-century illustrations also show adults playing the game.

Battledores would originally have been made from solid wood, but in later centuries they consisted of a wooden frame covered with vellum. Shapes and sizes varied considerably. Shuttlecocks consisted originally of feathers stuck into a cork base, and may have originated from the habit of storing quill feathers for writing, using the cork like a modern-day pen pot. In early shuttles, the cork would be lead-weighted and covered in leather, and the feathers would be from a goose or a chicken. In the nineteenth century, shuttlecocks were larger and heavier than modern ones, probably because they were designed to be used outdoors. Nowadays, in the modern sport of badminton, many shuttles are made from synthetic materials, but the best shuttles are still made from feathers – specifically from the left wing of a goose – and sixteen feathers are used in each shuttle. Shuttlecocks are also known as 'birdies' or 'birds' and their weight may vary from 4.74 to 5.5 grams.

Unlike badminton, the game of battledore and shuttlecock did not require the use of a net. Rather, the pastime could be played anywhere and at any time, which perhaps contributed to its popularity.

There was also an ancient game of 'shuttlecock' that was played with the feet, although there is a difference in opinion as to whether the feet were used to lift the shuttle into the air – as a racket – or whether this game was actually a form of football. Such games are depicted on Chinese pottery from around three thousand years ago, and evolved as an ancient military exercise. Chinese children still play shuttlecock or 'football of the feather' today.

Battledore and shuttlecock remained popular until the end of the nineteenth century, when it became overtaken by the game of badminton.

BADMINTON

B ADMINTON is a game for two or four players that involves the use of lightweight, stringed rackets, shuttle-cocks, and a net. Although now largely played indoors as an all-year-round sport, it is the perfect garden game for a balmy summer's day, and, even when played at a basic level and with the cheapest of equipment, can be a source of great fun and much enjoyment.

The sport of badminton is played on a marked-out court, which should be 44 feet (13.4 metres) long by 17 feet (5.2 metres) wide for the singles game, and 20 feet (6.1 metres) wide for the doubles. For those playing as a garden game, a court which is a little shorter and a little less wide can be easily forgiven, and, as the point of the game is that the shuttlecock should stay in the air and that every shot should be a volley, the less than smooth surface of an average lawn will not interfere too much with play. The net should be positioned correctly, however. It should sit across the centre of the court at a height of 5 feet (1.52 metres) from the ground at the middle and 5 feet 1 inch

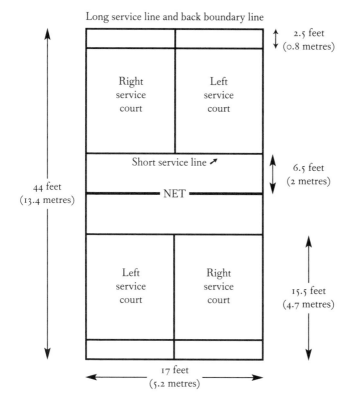

Long service line and back boundary line

2.5 feet (0.8 metres)

Right service court

Left service court

Short service line ↗

6.5 feet (2 metres)

NET

44 feet (13.4 metres)

Left service court

Right service court

15.5 feet (4.7 metres)

17 feet (5.2 metres)

Badminton singles court

(1.55 metres) at the net posts, and should be 2 feet 6 inches (0.76 metres) in depth.

To enjoy a good garden game of badminton it is best to choose a calm, windless day on which to play, and ideally to use the heaviest grade of shuttlecocks in order to prevent the shuttlecock from being blown off course, thus spoiling play.

Badminton is a simple game for beginners to grasp, as soon as one is accustomed to the flight of the shuttlecock and able to hit it cleanly. However, there is a whole range of strokes

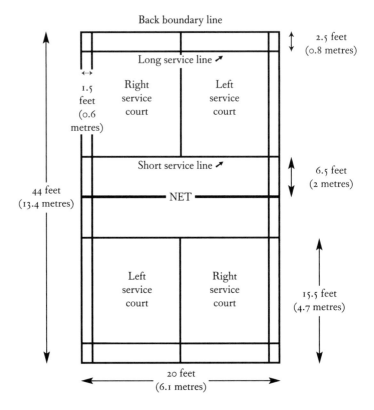

Badminton doubles court

and tactics waiting to be mastered if one wishes to play well. Those keen to win matches will need to familiarize themselves with the game's two most important strokes, the drop shot and the smash. It is worth noting that badminton is the world's fastest racket sport; a shuttle can leave the racket at a speed of almost 200 mph (322 kph). The game also rewards fitness; an energetic badminton player can cover more than a mile running about the court in a single match.

The basic rules of the game are that players should hit the shuttlecock back and forth over the net with their rackets until a shot is either not returned or is hit out of court. One player should act as server – the serve should be underarm – and the other as the receiver. Points are only awarded to the server or, in the case of doubles, the serving side. When the server loses a point, he relinquishes his serve to his opponent and becomes the receiver. However, in doubles, both players on the serving side must serve before play passes to the receivers, except on commencement of the game, when only one serve is permitted.

A game is played to 15 points, except in women's singles, which is played to 11 points. Generally, a match consists of the best of three games. If a game score reaches 14–14, the side that first reached 14 can choose either to end the set at 15 or play on to reach 17 points (known as 'setting'). In women's games and mixed doubles there is a 'setting' option to play the game to 13 when a game reaches 10–10.

The toss of the racket – one side is rough, the other smooth – determines who serves first. The winner of the toss can choose either to serve or to receive in the first game *or* which end to play from first. The loser has second choice. The server and receiver stand diagonally opposite during the service, but can then move anywhere on their side of the net. The service is served from the right at the start of the game and the receiver must stand still until the service is struck. (In doubles, only the person in the designated service area may return the serve.)

If the receiver fails to return the serve, the server wins a point – providing that the shuttlecock lands on or inside the lines making up the rectangle diagonally opposite the server. If the server wins a point, the next serve is then served from the left. In singles and doubles, the player/team who wins the first game, serves first in the second, and players change ends at the end of a game and also, in the case of the third game, when the leading score reaches 8 in a game of 15 points and 6 in a game of 11 points.

A rally is won if the shuttle is hit *over* the net and on to the floor of the opposing side's court, providing the shot is in court. A rally is lost if the shuttle is hit into the net or under the net, or if a receiving player hits the shuttle before it crosses the net. A rally is also lost if the shuttle touches a player or their clothing, and, of course, if a player fails to hit the shuttlecock, or hits it out of court. A shot falling on the line is in, and it is permissible to hit the shuttlecock with the wood or metal part of the racket. If the shuttlecock hits the net on the serve and still goes into the correct service court, play continues.

No one is completely sure how the game of badminton originated, but it is certain that it began to take shape in the 1800s. One theory is that it derives from a game played in India. British Army officers stationed there during the nineteenth century enjoyed a pastime known as Poona, which is similar to badminton. As they returned, some sought to establish Poona as an English game, so its popularity may have spread from here. Others believe that badminton evolved from battledore, and that as rackets became more sophisticated, so did the game. Interestingly, some early games appear to have been played with balls stuffed with feathers, rather than with shuttlecocks.

Indisputedly, badminton takes its name from Badminton House, the Gloucestershire seat of the Duke of Beaufort. Popular history has it that, in 1873, the Duke hosted a party here, and that due to the inclement weather the guests were in need of indoor entertainment. One guest had the idea of tying a string across the middle of a room, over which shuttlecocks were hit back and forth with the children's battle-dores. Thus a 'net' and opposite sides were introduced to battledore, and from that day 'The Game of Badminton' was estab-lished. However, a London toy dealer had published a booklet entitled 'Badminton Battledore – a new game' in 1860, while other accounts have it that this 'new game' was enjoyed at Badminton as early as the 1850s. It is even possible that the Indian game was played here, and thus took the name of the house.

Certainly badminton became a popular recreation for Englishmen between the 1860s and 1880s. Whereas all sexes had played battledore, interestingly the game was not deemed suitable for women initially. Its advantages as a garden game were that it could be played on even a small lawn, and that, as the shuttlecock did not need to bounce, the lawn need not be studiously maintained, or completely flat.

Although it did not capture the public imagination as quickly as lawn tennis, its popularity continued to grow, and in the 1880s the need for a fixed set of rules became apparent (until then, these had been largely open to interpretation). In 1887, a group of players formed the Bath Badminton Club and the rules of play became standardized. Then, in 1893, the Badminton Association was created to govern the sport, so that, for the first time, the same set of rules was adopted at a national level.

As more clubs became established, badminton became competitive, and championships began to be organized. In March 1898, the first open badminton tournament was held at Guildford, Surrey, and the first Open English Championship was held a year later on 4 April, at the headquarters of the London Scottish Rifles at Buckingham Gate, London. By the turn of the century women too were keen players, and, in 1900, a tournament for women was arranged. The first official All-England Championship was held in 1904, and by 1920 there were 300 English badminton clubs, rising to 9,000 throughout the British Isles by 1950. Badminton had grown from a gentleman's leisure activity into a serious sport.

Badminton's popularity had also spread abroad and in 1934 the International Badminton Federation (IBF) was created including the following member countries: England, Wales, Ireland, Scotland, Denmark, Holland, Canada, New Zealand and France. The United States also had many keen badminton players. Indeed the Badminton Club of the City of New York, which was established in 1878, is the oldest existing badminton club in the world, and the first US championships, played in Chicago in 1937, were played on twenty-one courts.

In March 1939, the IBF inaugurated an international competition and its president, Sir George Thomas, offered a trophy for the winning team. However, the first Thomas Cup matches had to be delayed until 1948 due to wartime lack of funds and shortages of shuttlecocks. Funding was still a sensitive issue in 1950, when it was decided that there would not be sufficient money to host a women's international competition.

The women's tournament was eventually established on a triennial basis, and the first tournament was held during 1956. Mrs H. S. Uber donated the trophy, and the tournament has been known as the Uber Cup ever since. The first fully professional open badminton tournament was played at the Royal Albert Hall, in London, in 1979.

Today the sport has a very busy calendar. There are now 147 member countries of the IBF and world events include the Uber Cup (ladies only), World Championships, Sudirman Cup (mixed team), World Juniors, World Grand Prix Finals, the World Cup and the Olympics. Badminton was admitted as a full medal sport at the Barcelona Olympics in 1992 and more than 1.1 billion people watched the televised coverage.

BOWLS

B owls is a splendid pastime. In theory it is simple to play, the basic idea being to roll balls (the bowls or 'woods') to a smaller white target ball called the jack. In essence, the game requires one to position the bowls as close as possible to the jack and to prevent one's opponent from doing so by blocking the path to the jack, moving the jack, or dislodging one's opponent's bowls.

A flat and well-groomed lawn may be considered best for play, but even in formal games there is disagreement on the subject of what constitutes a perfect 'green'. In the game of crown green bowls, for example, the green is actually on a slight slope.

To start a game, players take turns to bowl the jack until it stops in a position deemed suitable to bowl at. A toss of a coin will already have decided who is to bowl first. Players then take turns to roll their woods towards the jack, the winner being the person whose bowl comes closest.

Players may also team up, and in this case a more tactical game can be played, with some bowls aimed so as to knock opponents' bowls as far away from the jack as possible, or to block the jack so that the next bowler cannot reach it easily. The winning team scores a point for each wood that is closer to the jack than the opposing team's closest wood. The overall winner is the first to reach an agreed number of points, which should be decided on before the start of play.

Bowls is one of the oldest outdoor pastimes, but there is some argument surrounding its history, and it is hard to pin down a point in time at which the game separated from others involving objects aimed at a target. In England, for instance, a game called 'Knock-the-devil-down', in which peasants lined up several clubs and then knocked them down by throwing round stones at them, is said to be an early form of bowls, as is loggets, a game in which small pieces of wood were pitched at a stake in the ground, the nearest thrower winning. A very similar game to loggets was also played with bones. In medieval times, there existed a game called Jacti Lapidum, which also involved throwing stones at a target, and it is possible that the bowling term 'jack' derives from this game.

Before this, ancient civilizations are known to have practised games involving throwing objects at a target. Roman soldiers played a game that involved throwing stones at a target stone, while artefacts in Egyptian tombs dating from 5,000 BC tell a similar story. The Mongols and the Aztecs are even supposed to have played a bowls-type game with their enemies' heads.

Some like to believe that bowls was brought to England by William the Conqueror in 1066, and that it derives from the French game of 'boules'. However, there is a Saxon word 'bolla', so perhaps the English already had their own version of the game when William arrived. Really, however, these histories can be applied to any of the bowls-type games that are played today, whether bowls, boules, skittles, ninepins, or pétanque.

It is notable that in all of these early games, objects were thrown rather than rolled. Even when the first proper bowling greens became established, throwing may still have been the common form of play. Without the

advantages of lawnmowers, which were not invented until 1832, the greens would have been cut with a scythe, and therefore would probably have been uneven, making it hard to roll a stone or ball across them.

Interestingly, bowling was one of the first sports for which proper playing areas were created. Initially these were mostly exclusive to the upper classes or to the church and could be found within the precincts of monasteries or castles. Some were available for public play, however. The oldest bowling green is thought to be that of the Southampton Town Bowling Club, which was founded in 1299.

By the fourteenth century, the English population had embraced bowls with great enthusiasm – so much so that, in 1366, Edward III had a law passed forbidding play, because he feared that people were not keeping to archery practice. With the threat of battle always a possibility, even in peacetime, all men over a certain age were supposed to practise archery. People must have continued to play in spite of this, for two decades later Richard II renewed these laws.

However, kings could exempt themselves from the laws they passed. Henry VIII was certainly a keen bowler. He not only built a bowling alley at Whitehall, but he also incurred large losses betting on the game, even wagering on his own skill when he played. He preferred his subjects to occupy themselves more usefully, though. Therefore, when it was brought to his attention that 'Bowyers, Fletchers, Stringers and Arrowhead makers' were spending working hours at the bowling green, he too imposed a ban on the sport.

In 1511, he reasserted the existing laws prohibiting play (in fact, the first officially documented version of the word 'bowls' occurs in this statute), and by an act of 1541, artificers, labourers, apprentices, servants and the like were forbidden from playing bowls at any time except Christmas, and then only in their master's house and presence. It was also forbidden for anyone to 'play at any bowle or bowles in open space out of his own garden or orchard', and those caught doing so were liable to a fine of 6s. 8d. Only those possessed of lands of the yearly value of £100 could obtain licences to play on their own private greens.

Additionally, a total ban was imposed on play at public bowling alleys. As bowling had become popular, many alehouses had created a bowling green or alley on their premises. Thus the public game had become associated with drunkenness, gambling and low behaviour, and the authorities had been quick to disapprove. The aristocratic game was held to be free from such association, although certainly all classes gambled on play. And it was not only common citizens who grew rowdy during a game of bowls, for John Aylmer, the sixteenth-century bishop of London, evidently used language during a match 'as justly exposed his character to reproach'.

Probably the most famous, although possibly apocryphal game of bowls is the one played by Sir Francis Drake at Plymouth Hoe, in 1588. England had been at war with Spain for many years, and Drake, then second-in-command of the English fleet, had wanted to mount an offensive against the

Spanish Armada before it left Spain. However, by the time his plans were approved, the Spanish ships were close to English shores. So the story goes, on Sunday 19 June, Drake was playing bowls on the hoe when news reached him that the Spanish Armada had been sighted in the English Channel. Drake's companions made as if to finish the game,  but he continued to play, uttering the words, 'There is plenty of time to win this game, and to thrash the Spaniards too.' He actually went on to lose the game, but did roundly beat the Spanish. It is said that Drake played his game with cannon balls.

The evolution of the bowling ball is an interesting one. First round stones were used, and later most people played with solid wood balls. Iron balls were also experimented with (hence, perhaps Drake's cannon balls), but the wooden type prevailed, especially as the invention of the power lathe allowed for more regular wooden bowling balls. Lignum vitae, a hard tropical wood, was popularly used for making bowls until recently. Today, most balls are made from hard rubber, or a compound material. Usually they have a diameter of between 4.7 and 5.7 inches (12 and 14.5 centimetres) and a weight of between 3 and 3.5 lbs (1360 and 1580 grams). The jack must be round and white with a diameter of about 2.5 inches (6.25 cm) and a weight of between 0.5 and 0.63 lbs (227 and 284 grams).

The first documented use of the word 'jack' is said to date from 1611. It is thought that in certain contexts 'jack' may mean a slightly smaller version of something. In 1697, one

R. Pierce wrote, 'He had not strength to throw the Jack-Bowl half over the Green'.

In the sixteenth century the biased bowl was introduced, which is now essential to the game. In 1556, Robert Recorde, a mathematician, wrote, 'A little altering of the one side maketh the bowl to run biases waies'. William Shakespeare also wrote about biased bowls; in his play *Richard II*, the queen's response to her lady's suggestion that a game of bowls might relieve her boredom is: ''Twill make me think the world is full of rubs, and that my fortune runs against the bias.' There is a story that the Duke of Suffolk was the first to play with a biased bowl. Supposedly, during a game, his bowl split into two halves. Not to be thwarted by this, he ran indoors and sawed the spherical knob off the banister in the grand hall of the house at which he was playing. The flat bottom of his new bowl, however, made it run in an arc, which he soon discovered improved his play as he had a better view of the jack.

As the widespread use of banister knobs was a far from practical solution to creating a biased bowl, the same effect was initially achieved by drilling a hole into one side of the bowl and loading it with lead or a weight. Today's bowls all have a certain amount of bias, but are deliberately crafted so that they are not quite round, with one side being more convex than the other, and the slight bulge showing the side with the bias. When a ball is moving quickly, it travels in a straight line, but as it slows down the extra weight on the bulging side makes it begin to roll in the direction of the bias. A bowler can therefore make the ball curve in one direction or the other by positioning the bias correctly. In some bowling games the jack is also biased, although not in all.

The Stuart kings James I and Charles I both found bowls an enjoyable pastime, but whereas the former recommended a moderate indulgence, the latter played the game to excess, encouraging wagering and playing for high stakes, so that the bowling greens of the upper classes gained as bad a reputation as those of common bowling alleys. It was said of Charles that he 'drank from the bowl, and bowl'd for what he drank'. However, under Puritan rule, such behaviour was suppressed, and for a time bowls all but ceased to be played in England. Even after the Restoration of 1660, the game did not achieve its former popularity, and as populations in towns began to increase, many city bowling greens were demolished to make way for new buildings.

However, during Cromwell's rule, bowls did travel to the New World. A bowling green in Williamsburg, Virginia, was created in 1632, for example, and one in New York City in 1732. George Washington was known to play bowls on his estate. By the early 1700s, bowls was being played in Canada, and also in Australia by the mid-1800s.

Bowls also flourished in Scotland where every town was said to have a green. In fact, such was the enthusiasm for the game that, in 1848, 200 members of Scottish Bowling clubs congregated in Glasgow Town Hall, where they appointed W. W. Mitchell to draw up a uniform code of laws to govern the game. Thus the first standardized rules and regulations were set down.

In the late 1800s and early 1900s, several independent bowls associations were set up both in Britain and abroad, with the intention of regularizing the game. However, this in itself proved contradictory, as various regions played by different rules. Today, bowls still takes several forms, although the basic rules are applicable to all. In England, for example, lawn or flat green bowls is popular in the South, while crown green bowls is popular in the North, the games having variations in equipment and in the type of green on which they are played.

Bowls is now played in over thirty-five countries, and is presided over by the World Bowling Board, which is responsible for the standardization of rules across the world.

BOULES

Boules is an excellent garden game, as not only can it played by players aged eight to eighty, but it suits most garden areas, even those not in France.

Boules is the generic term for a number of similar bowls-type games. As in the game of bowls, the objective is to get one's balls or boules closer to the jack than anyone else's, but boules can be played on any surface – gravel, sand, grass – and the metal balls are much smaller, being just larger than a cricket ball.

The jack, which is also known as the 'cochonnet' (piglet in French) is made of wood and is similar in size to a table-tennis ball. Normally a tool called a 'baguette' is used to measure the distance between boules closest to the jack, and thus to settle any arguments.

There are various games one can play with boules. It is a team game with the singles known as 'tête-à-tête', the doubles as 'doublettes', and the triples as 'triplettes'. In the first two, players have three boules, while in 'triplettes' each player has two. It is important that teams have the same number of boules. Only informal games can include four players in a team.

A toss of the coin determines which team will bowl first. At the start of the game a circle is drawn on the ground and this is where each player has to stand to take their throw. A member of the team that won the toss both chooses the starting place, and draws the circle. The first ball thrown is the cochonnet which must land 6.5–11 yards (6–10 metres) from the circle, be visible from the circle, and must not be too close to any obstacles such as trees or garden fences. In some boules games the playing area is delimited – usually a long, thin strip with marked or boarded edges. In others the game is played over a large flat area.

One player from each team then proceeds to throw a boule, with the team that won the toss throwing both the cochonnet and the first boule. Shots can be played either with the aim of getting close to the jack or tactically to ruin opponents' chances of doing so. The second bowler must decide whether he will try to beat the first bowler's attempt at getting near to the cochonnet, or whether it might be more to his team's advantage to move the first boule from its resting position. The best shot is when one's ball lands squarely upon an opponent's boule in such a way that the opponent's ball shoots off, while one's own takes its place. This is known as a 'carreau'.

The boule deemed nearest to the cochonnet is called the 'best boule', and the team that owns it is said to be 'holding'. The first bowl is obviously the 'best boule'. If the second bowl becomes 'best boule', the first team then bowls again, each team member taking turns to throw, and continuing to do so until they have either used all their boules, or they get a boule closest to the jack. Then the other team throws, and so on.

When both teams have no more boules the points are counted, with the winning team getting a point for each boule that is closer to the jack than the losing team's boules. The game consists of a number of 'ends', an 'end' being over when each team has thrown all its boules. After this a player from the winning team throws the cochonnet from where it rests and the game starts again until one team reaches a score of thirteen points.

As team members start to display their skill at the game, they may take on specific roles. The 'milieu', for example, is the captain, and should be a good all-round player. The 'pointeur' is the person best at getting boules nearest to the cochonnet, and for this reason the pointeur will often bowl first. The 'tireur' or 'bomber', meanwhile, has the job of knocking the opposition's boules out of play.

The boules themselves vary in size, weight, pattern and materials, and regular players usually form a preference for one sort over another. The best boules are made from stainless steel, although a set of plastic boules is good enough for play in the garden. However, once one has played with the stainless steel variety there is no comparison, and it might be worth paying a little more for such a set.

Like bowls, boules also derives from ancient times, perhaps from the Egyptians, or from the ancient Greeks who played a game with round stones, or the Romans who played a game with small wooden balls covered in iron. It is thought that while the Greeks enjoyed competing for who could throw a stone over the furthest distance, Roman players preferred aiming at a target ball – indeed, it is likely that the Romans were the inventors of the jack.

The Romans probably introduced the game to France around 600 BC when they captured Marseilles and Lyon, and the game gradually spread across the country. It is said to take its name from the French word boulevard, meaning leafy avenue, and in the Middle Ages, players became known as 'bouleurs'.

The various types of boules games are thought to have resulted from bans placed on the game by those in authority. If the game was banned under one name, it was simply given another, and in this way play could continue. Often boules games carry regional titles such as *jeu provençal* – 'the game of Provence', or *lyonnaise*, which became the game associated with Lyon and surrounding areas.

Interestingly, in 1629, it was the manufacturers of a rival game, the early tennis game known as 'paumes', that had boules banned. However, their attempts to suppress the game were short-lived, for boules lovers simply ignored it.

Lyonnaise is probably the oldest of the boules games played in France, but today it is the game of pétanque, established in 1910, that has become the boules game of choice. So the story goes, a popular bowler by the name of Jules Le Noir suffered from rheumatism, which left him wheelchair bound. As the local game of jeu provençal involved taking a run up of one or two paces to the throwing circle, he was forced to spectate rather than participate in the game he loved.

Being sympathetic to his plight, his friends therefore decided to bend the rules somewhat, and devised a new way of playing in which the bowler kept both feet within the bowling circle while delivering a ball. Thus, the game of *pieds tanqués* or 'feet together' first came to be played, which is known today as pétanque. The game is also played over a shorter distance than jeu provençal. It quickly became popular, and by 1935, there were 135,000 registered players. However, the French National Boule Federation, who supported lyonnaise (which is played with a larger and heavier boule than is used in pétanque and is also played on a clearly marked piste), refused to recognize pétanque, so that, in 1945, a rival federation was set up jointly by players of pétanque and jeu provençal.

Today pétanque is also popular in Britain, although it did not take off here until after the Second World War. Worldwide it is thought to have more players than any other outdoor bowling game, with 600,000 registered players in forty-six countries.

CRICKET

CRICKET is a team game involving skills with a bat and a ball. Believed to have originated in the thirteenth century, the game played today is a popular summer sport in Britain, in gardens, parks, amateur leagues, professional county leagues, and on the international stage. There are many rules associated with this great sport, but for the purpose of simply enjoying a fun game in the garden or park, a selection of only the basic rules and playing styles follows.

On a full-size cricket pitch, a total of eleven players per team take part, but in the garden, within a far smaller playing area, teams of five or six would be more appropriate. In the middle of the lawn, the batting and bowling area known as the 'wicket' must be marked out, using tape or string. An official wicket has a length of 22 yards (20.1 metres) and a bowling crease width of 8 feet 8 inches yards (2.64 metres), but it would be acceptable to reduce the size of the wicket in proportion to the size of the lawn. At each end of the length of the wicket, three slim poles known as the 'stumps', each with a height of 28 inches (71.1 centimetres), are inserted into the ground in a straight line, along the width of the wicket, at a total width of 9 inches (22.9 centimetres). After the stumps

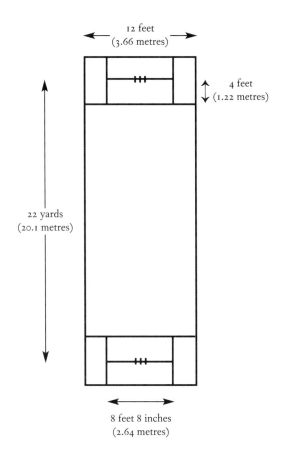

12 feet
(3.66 metres)

4 feet
(1.22 metres)

22 yards
(20.1 metres)

8 feet 8 inches
(2.64 metres)

Cricket pitch

have been lined up accurately, two shorter sticks known as the 'bails', each with a length of 4.38 inches (11.1 centimetres) are placed on top of the stumps. The rest of the surrounding area of grass is called the 'outfield'.

An official cricket ball is made up of cork and twine on the interior, covered by quarters of red leather stitched together.

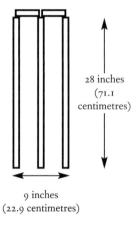

28 inches
(71.1
centimetres)

9 inches
(22.9 centimetres)

Cricket wicket

It is not advisable to use such a hard ball in a simple game of garden cricket; a tennis ball would suffice. The maximum length of a cricket bat (made of willow and fitted with a rubber-covered grip) is 38 inches (96.5 centimetres), with a maximum width of 4.25 inches (10.8 centimetres).

Before a game of cricket begins, a simple toss of a coin decides who will bat or field first. At any one time, there are two batters from Team One standing on the wicket, one in front of each set of stumps and bails (also known collectively as the 'wicket', perhaps confusingly). The remaining team members are onlookers, waiting for their turn to bat. Team Two comprises of the fielding side, individuals who occupy different areas of the pitch, in preparation for catching or retrieving the ball if it is hit in their direction. The batter stands just in front of the stumps and bails, within the batting area called the 'crease', and tries to hit the ball after it is bowled, in order to score 'runs'. At the same time, the bowler, from the opposing team, is trying to get the batsman 'out'. Put simply, a run is scored when the batter hits the ball into the outfield, and he and his batting partner both run from one end of the wicket to the other, before the ball is thrown back to the stumps by a fielder.

The batters can run between the wickets as many times as possible until the ball is thrown back to the wicket, and for every complete run, the batter who hit the ball earns a point for his team called a 'run'. An automatic 'four' runs are awarded if the ball is hit into the outfield and bounces at least once along the ground before crossing the edge of the pitch, known as the 'boundary'. A score of 'six' runs is awarded if the ball is hit over the boundary without bouncing at all. Thus, the object of the game for the first batting team is to score as many runs as possible. In the meantime, the fielding team is focused on getting each of the batting team 'out'. This can be achieved in a number of ways: 'caught out' – when the ball is hit by the batter and is caught directly (without bouncing) by a fielder; 'bowled out' – when the bowler throws a ball that the batsman misses, and it hits and dislodges the stumps

or bails; 'run out' – when the batters are running between the wickets, and the fielding side throw the ball at the stumps, and hit them before the batter reaches the crease; the 'leg before wicket rule' (lbw) – when the batter does not play a stroke, and the ball hits a part of his leg directly in line with the wicket, which would have hit the stumps or bails had his leg not been in the way; 'stumped' – when the wicketkeeper (the fielder who stands behind the stumps and bails), catches a ball that the batter may have missed and touches the stumps or bails with the ball, when the batter is standing out of his crease; 'hit wicket' – when the batter takes a swing at the ball, but misses and hits the stumps or bails instead.

A bowler has six opportunities to throw the ball at the batter in front of one of the wickets. These six attempts are collectively known as an 'over'. However, if the bowler throws the ball wildly or inaccurately, a 'no-ball' will be called, and the batting team earns a free run, while the bowler must throw the ball again. A batter can also score runs if the ball bounces past him without him hitting it, and he runs between the wickets (called a 'bye') or if the ball bounces off his leg without touching the bat (called a 'leg-bye'), but for the purposes of playing cricket in the garden, these technical terms can be ignored. After the first over, a different bowler will bowl towards the batter standing in front of the other wicket, and the bowling alternates in this fashion until all members of the batting team are out, or until a certain number of overs have been bowled.

In an official game of cricket, the bowler throws the ball in an overarm motion, swinging the ball over his head and bringing it down so it bounces in front of the batter. However, in a game of cricket in the garden, it would be perfectly acceptable to bowl using a more straightforward under-arm motion.

When all but one of the batting team have been declared out, it is the end of the innings, and the fielding team become the batting team and vice versa. The winning team is the team that has scored the most runs. In professional and amateur one-day games of cricket, there can be a limited number of overs bowled per team, but in games played in the garden, teams can choose to play until each team has batted and fielded once, and the resulting scores of runs have been added up. It is important to keep careful track of the number of runs scored, to avoid any disagreements at the end of the match!

The origins of cricket are shrouded in mystery, but many theories about its history abound. In the thirteenth century a pastime similar to cricket by the name of 'creag' was played in parts of Kent. Indeed sixteen-year-old Prince Edward, the future Edward II, was said to have played 'creag' with his companion Piers Gaveston in 1300. Similarly, 'club-ball', a game which involved the batter defending a hole in the ground, was played at the same time as 'creag'.

The first proven written reference to cricket being played in England appears in a legal document dated 16 January 1598, which referred to the schooldays of a man in Guildford, during which he would 'runne and play . . . at krickett and other plaies'.

Early bats were little more than sticks until the distinctive curved design of the modern bat gradually developed. Before the first proper seamed cricket ball was made in 1775, cricket in its infancy was played using pieces of wood and stones of varying sizes, though by the seventeenth century balls were being constructed by interlacing strips of hide together.

The game grew in popularity throughout the south-eastern counties during Charles II's reign. Royal patronage of the sport continued with King George II's son, Prince Frederick, who was an ardent promoter of cricket, while the future George IV was an equally enthusiastic player and supporter of the game. The first recorded cricket match in England took place in Coxheath, Kent, in 1646, during which the first instance of betting on the game was also recorded.

As more and more cricket clubs began to spring up throughout Kent, Surrey and a number of other southern counties, it was decided that a set of rules was needed to regulate and the game, and so the first Code of Laws was drawn up in 1744, devised by members of the 'London Club'. These laws were subsequently revised in 1755 and 1774, by a number of individuals who would later become members of the Marylebone Cricket Club (MCC), which was established in 1787 as a consequence of the increasing popularity of the sport among royalty and the nobility. The MCC would play a significant role in the future administration of cricket at both domestic and international level.

Under the first Code of Laws, the width of the 'batte' was limited to 4.5 inches (11.4 centimetres), and the weight of the ball was restricted to 5–6 ounces (142–170 grams). Originally a wicket was made up of only two stumps; a third stump was introduced to a match in London in 1775, and ten years later three stumps became standard. Similarly, early wickets had only a single bail; the notion of two bails per wicket was first suggested in 1786.

By the mid-nineteenth century, cricket was becoming widely played in the North of England and the Midlands, resulting in the formation of first-class county cricket leagues. Indeed the first county championship table was published in 1864. It was at this time that county cricket was growing in importance and in quality, producing skilful and talented players such as the great W. G. Grace, who, over a forty-three-year, first-class career scored 54,896 runs and took 2,864 wickets.

W. G. Grace

As Englishmen left their country to settle abroad, they continued to play their beloved game of cricket on foreign soil, thereby introducing the sport to a host of new nations. In 1859 the first English cricket team to play abroad embarked on a tour across Canada and the USA, playing (and winning) their first game in Montreal. Cricket also became popular on the other side of the globe in Australia, and in 1877, the first Test match between England and Australia was played in Melbourne, in which the home team was victorious. Thus began a rivalry between the two nations that still exists to this day. Since 1882, the prize at stake in Test matches between England and Australia has been a tiny urn containing the 'Ashes'. The Ashes story began the day after the England cricket team was beaten by Australia in London, in August 1882, when the *Sporting Times* newspaper printed the following tongue-in-cheek obituary: 'In affectionate remembrance of English Cricket which died at The Oval on 29th August 1882. Deeply lamented by a large circle of sorrowing friends and acquaintances. RIP. NB – The body will be cremated and the ashes taken to Australia.' Months later, on the 1882–3

England tour of Australia, some ladies from Melbourne were said to have burned a cricket bail, and placed the resulting ashes into a wooden urn, which was later presented to the England captain, the Honourable Ivo Bligh. On his death in 1927 he bequeathed the ashes to the MCC, and to this day they are the token trophy played for by the English and Australian Test teams in memory of the 1882 match.

By the twentieth century the MCC remained an influential and powerful body in English cricketing circles, and in 1903, was responsible for the selection and administration of all England's overseas tours. The Imperial Cricket Conference was founded in 1909, by individuals representing cricket in England, Australia and South Africa. Subsequent nations to be made full members of the ICC (later renamed the International Cricket Council) were India, West Indies and New Zealand in 1926, Pakistan in 1952, Sri Lanka in 1981 and Zimbabwe in 1992.

Today the sport has a busy domestic calendar in England and Wales, with two divisions containing nine teams playing four-day county championships games, the same eighteen teams playing one-day National Cricket League games and one-day Cup matches, while internationally, overseas tours incorporating five-day Test series' are played throughout the world, as well as series' of one-day international matches (since 1971) and a World Cup tournament held once every four years (since 1975).

The game of cricket has spread far and wide across the globe from Australia to Zimbabwe, and continues to be enjoyed in gardens, parks and on village greens throughout Britain, during the summer months.

CROQUET

ROQUET is perhaps the quintessential English garden game, a natural partner to sultry afternoons, strawberries and Pimm's. Like all great garden games it can be as simple or as tactically complex as the skill and experience of the players dictate.

Broadly speaking, the aim of the game is go around a course of hoops staked out in the garden twice, first one way and then another, before hitting a centre peg with each of one's balls, 'pegging out', and therefore winning the game. There is not a complete set of standard regulations to govern

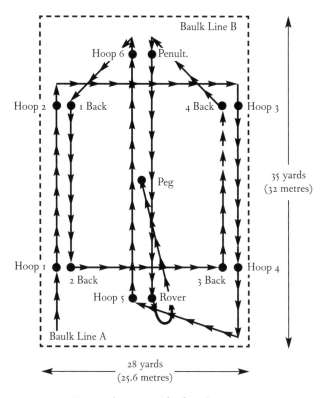

Croquet lawn: standard setting

play, but the most widely played version of croquet is the International Association Croquet singles game. There are separate rules for doubles, the American game, and the American garden game.

A basic croquet set comprises six hoops, one peg, four mallets and four balls, coloured black and blue (the cold colours), and red and yellow (the hot colours). The better sets will also include four hoop clips of matching colour to indicate the next target for each ball, a small mallet for hammering the hoops and peg into the ground, four corner flags, and eight corner pegs to mark the ends of the four yard-lines.

The ideal playing surface should be a level and pristine lawn, but for most cases a largish grass area will suffice, provided the grass is not made up of impenetrable undergrowth. The standard croquet lawn measures 35 by 28 yards (32 by 25.6 metres) and is delineated by a white line. The four edges of the lawn are referred to by the four compass points, but these are determined by croquet etiquette and not the Pole, with South always being the boundary facing the first hoop.

A peg is erected in the precise centre of the lawn and the six hoops are positioned relative to the peg. Hoops all face North and South (croquet not magnetic compass points again) and Hoop 5 is positioned 7 yards (6.4 metres) north of the peg and the last hoop, known as 'the Rover' is 7 yards south of the peg. The first hoop is placed 7 yards in from the South boundary and 7 yards in from the West boundary and the remaining three hoops are similarly placed near each corner, each one 7 yards in from its two respective boundaries. Do not worry: croquet is much more fun to play than it is to set up!

Hoops have to be passed in the correct order which is as follows:

Hoop 1	South-West corner	Northwards
Hoop 2	North-West corner	Northwards
Hoop 3	North-East corner	Southwards
Hoop 4	South-East corner	Southwards
Rover	Centre-South	Northwards
Hoop 5	Centre-North	Northwards

Balls are then played back in reverse direction as follows:

Hoop 2	North-West corner	Southwards
Hoop 1	South-West corner	Southwards
Hoop 4	South-East corner	Northwards
Hoop 3	North-East corner	Northwards
Hoop 5	Centre-North	Southwards
Rover	Centre-South	Southwards

'Pegging out' each ball marks the conclusion of the game.

Balls are played in pairs, the cold colours, black and blue, versus the hot colours, red and yellow. The balls are played in order – blue, red, black and finally yellow. After the fourth turn each turn starts with the player deciding which of the two balls to play. That ball is then played throughout the turn and the other ball is termed 'the partner ball'. A player keeps playing until a struck ball either fails to pass through a hoop (known as 'running the hoop') or to hit another ball (known as a 'roquet').

A roquet entitles a player to two extra strikes. The first of which is the eponymous 'croquet' shot where a player picks up a ball and places it so it touches the ball it came into contact with (the roqueted ball) and then strikes the first ball so that the roqueted ball also moves, either advantageously if it is his ball or into a dire position if it is his opponent's. The plosive sound of this shot is a possible source of the name croquet, which may be taken from the French *croquer*, meaning to crack. This

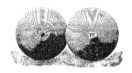

phase of the game is where it may become a little less genteel and a little more ruthless. A player may only roquet the other three balls once between each hoop during a turn. A further tactic involves 'peeling' the partner ball (where a player's first ball will attempt to strike the second ball through its own hoop).

The best players will try to make their turn last as long as possible, a little like an accomplished snooker player, a game which shares a common ancestry with croquet. In theory a turn can last until victory is achieved, a player running several hoops in one turn. An extended turn like this is, as in snooker, called a 'break' and if all twelve hoops are run in one turn a player is congratulated for achieving an 'all-round break'.

A simpler variation of the game, known as golf croquet, is also widely played. It is a good alternative for those too impatient to wait while others amass a lengthy break and does not include croquet shots. The objective is to score a set number of points for the side by hitting one's ball through the appropriate next hoop successfully, in a system similar to that employed by match-play golf. For many, just getting the ball through the hoops on a lumpy and divot-strewn lawn is a sufficient challenge in itself.

The history of croquet can be traced to Europe in the Middle Ages, where games would normally involve one ball struck though a very wide hoop. Thirteenth-century French peasants enjoyed whacking wooden balls through hoops made from willow branches. The French continued their love of this pastime well into the seventeenth century when *paille maille* was all the rage. The game was introduced to London and was played in open ground near St James's Palace, the area used for the pitch being known as 'The Mall' and the whole area as 'Pall Mall'. *Paille maille* was also akin to golf, given the distances involved, in this case 1,000 yards (914 metres), and the strokes required to propel the balls such a long way.

A game known as 'closh' was also played in England and Holland. References in English to either 'closh', 'cloish', 'claish' or 'clash' appear between 1477 to 1861, but its rules are somewhat opaque. Closh appears to be a fusion of skittles and lawn billiards. References from the sixteenth and seventeenth centuries imply that balls were directed through hoops or rings by a large spade-like instrument called a 'klos-beytel'.

In 1864, troco or lawn billiards was popular with discerning English gentlefolk, the object being to pass a wooden ball through an iron ring fixed on a movable pivot in the centre of

The eighteenth-century game of paille maille

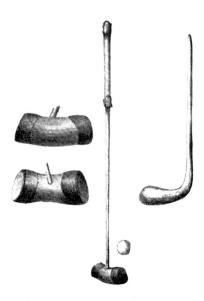

a circle around which players took their places. A cue with an iron ring was used to propel one's ball through the circle with one's opponents attempting to thwart its progress using a croquet-like roquet shot, also known as a 'canon'.

A game called 'crookey' was played in Ireland from the 1830s and was brought to England in 1852 where it soon caught on, partly because it was a game with equal appeal to both men and women. This principal of equality remains with the modern game of croquet, which employs a well-developed handicapping system. As in golf, once a newcomer to the sport has grasped the basics he will be given a handicap of about twenty-four. The best players will be on scratch or better. Each point on the handicap scales allows a player to claim a free turn (called a 'bisque') at any point during a game. This way croquet players in their prime, usually their mid-twenties and thirties, can play a novice on an equal footing.

Crinoline wearers were sometimes guilty of cheating at croquet

In the thirty years following its introduction to Britain, uniform rules for croquet and national competitions were established. The first national headquarters for the game was the Wimbledon All-England Croquet Club, which held the first national championship in Victorian times. Of course,

Wimbledon is now better known as the home of tennis, and this eclipsing of croquet by tennis was apparent worldwide by the 1900s.

However, it is worth remembering that the waning of croquet's popularity is relevant only on a competitive level. Croquet at club level is still incredibly strong, not only in England but also Australia, New Zealand and America, and croquet is played competitively in over twenty countries, while the number playing in gardens outstrips those playing in clubs tenfold.

FRENCH CRICKET

THIS is a simple game that can be played by all the family. Players take it in turns to hold a cricket bat or tennis racket, while another player bowls a tennis ball. The aim of the game is for the bowler to try to hit the batter's legs below the knee, and for the batter to defend himself from such onslaught by holding the bat or racket in front of his or her legs. If the batter's leg is hit, he or she is out. If the batter manages to hit the ball, however, he or she scores a point and has another turn in bat. The batter is also out if the fielding side catches the ball after it has been hit, without the ball bouncing, and the person who achieves such a catch becomes the next bowler.

If the batter has hit the ball, there is another bonus in being able to turn to face the new direction of the thrown ball. The ball must be bowled from where it either stops or is stopped by a fielder. If the batter has hit the ball, he is allowed to move his feet in order to best position himself to face the next ball. However, if he has failed to hit the ball, but remains in the game because his legs have not been hit, he is not allowed to reposition his feet, thus potentially being forced to reach the bat behind himself in order to protect his legs. If the batter misses the ball but inadvertently moves his feet then he will be forced to play 'sticks'. In this case the bat is inverted and the handle is used to defend one's legs until the batter hits the ball again or, and this is the more likely outcome, he is out.

FRISBEE

WHEN one thinks of a Frisbee, one tends to think of a brightly coloured plastic disk – a modern toy that can be much fun to play with once the throwing action has been mastered. In fact, though, the frisbee has quite a long history, and has its roots in the origin of pies, or rather, in pie tins.

In the 1870s, William Russell Frisbie opened a bakery called the Frisbie Pie Company in Bridgeport, Connecticut. Legend has it that in the mid-1940s, students at Yale University began to play a game of throw and catch with empty pie tins. These were embossed with the Frisbie Pie Company's name, and so the game became known as Frisbie. Some people have disputed the fact that it was pie tins that were thrown around, believing instead that it was cookie tins, which stored Frisbie's finest sugar cookies, that were the original prototype for the Frisbee.

Elsewhere in America, others lay claim to a similar story. In May 1989, Middlebury College in Vermont unveiled a bronze statue of a dog jumping to catch a Frisbee, allegedly to commemorate the Frisbee's fiftieth anniversary. According to them, in 1939, five undergraduates were driving through Nebraska when they got a flat tyre. While the tyre was being changed, those not involved went into a cornfield, where they found an empty Frisbie pie tin and began to throw it to each other. In fact, it would seem that all over America someone can lay claim to being the first to realize that Frisbie pie tins were as suited to the air as they were to the oven.

It appears that the Frisbie Company failed to realize the potential fortune they were sitting on, for they went out of business in 1958. Meanwhile, Walter Frederick Morrison, a Los Angeles building inspector, had noted Hollywood's obsession with UFOs. Thus, he designed a lightweight, plastic disk, based on the Frisbie pie tin, which he called a Flying Saucer. He sold the rights to the Wham-O Manufacturing Co. in California, and on 13 January 1957, it was launched across the USA.

In 1994, Wham-O was acquired by Mattel, and the name Frisbee is now a registered trademark. The popularity of the Frisbee is undiminished and in the USA alone more are sold each year than the collective sale of baseballs, basketballs and footballs.

Spin-offs games such as Freestyle Frisbee and Ultimate Frisbee are taken very seriously, with rules attached to play, and names for various throws and catches. There are a huge number of players and many competitions, including the World Frisbee Championships.

LAWN TENNIS

T ENNIS is a game for everyone, from the small child, learning to swing a racket, to older folk who like to keep on their toes; from the amateur to the expert; from the keen player to the keen spectator. Its basic rules are simple to learn, and, although the game is best played with good quality rackets, new balls, and on a well tended grass court, it need not be an expensive pastime and a rough approximation of a court will suffice for those with smaller gardens.

The thud of tennis balls goes hand in hand with the hazy, lazy days of an English summer and a large degree of nostalgia surrounds the game (some still refer to the 1920s as its heyday). It is a perfect sunny afternoon, players are engaging in pleasing rallies on the lawn, spectators are sipping cool lemonade and growing sleepy in the sun, and everyone is having fun. This idyll is one that we seek to preserve, and, no matter if the weather is still cold and wet, when tennis nets start to go up on outdoor courts, summer has arrived.

Historically, there have been twenty-four spellings of the word 'tennis', which derives from an old French custom of shouting 'tenez' (from the French verb *tenir*, meaning 'to hold') before serving. In practice, it is an energetic game, and a good player will be ready to volley at the net at one moment, and return a shot from the baseline at the next. At its most fundamental, tennis is played by two or four players on a large rectangular court with a net across the middle. Each player will need a tennis racket, and a supply of good balls.

Like badminton, lawn tennis should be played on a marked-out court, measuring 78 feet (23.8 metres) long by 27 feet (8.23 metres) wide for the singles game, and 36 feet (11 metres) wide for doubles. However, it is perfectly acceptable to play on a lawn that is a little shorter and a little narrower. The shorter the grass the better, as the balls will need to bounce smoothly in order to make the game as fair as possible. The net should be positioned across the centre of the court at a consistent height of 3.5 feet (1.07 metres) from the ground.

Players stand on opposite sides of the net and take up suitable positions for the start of play, depending on whether they are serving or receiving. The serving player stands with both feet behind the baseline at a point somewhere between the middle of the baseline and the sideline. When the receiver is ready, the server throws a ball into the air with his hand, and, as the ball descends and before it makes contact with the ground, hits it with his racket in such a way that it travels diagonally across the court, over the net, and lands either within or on the lines marking the service box. The server must remain with at least one foot on the ground behind the baseline during delivery. Once over the net, the ball must be allowed to bounce once before the opponent attempts to return it.

If the serve is hard and fast enough, the receiver may fail to return the ball. This is called an 'ace' and, if no 'fault' has occurred during delivery, the server wins a point. If the serve is returned, however, a rally may commence, with play continuing until one player misses the ball or hits it either into the net or 'out', outside of the court. The winning player gains a point. (Common shots employed in a rally are the 'forehand', the 'backhand', and the 'volley' – a ball that is returned to an opponent before it bounces.) If a server fails to get the ball into the service box on the first serve, this is classed as a fault and he is allowed to serve again. If he still fails to serve the ball into the service box, this is a 'double fault', and the point goes to his opponent. If the ball either hits or clips the net during one of these shots, it is known as a 'let', and the server is allowed to retake the serve. The server continues to serve for the rest of the game, but from alternate sides – that is right and left-hand side – of the court. With the start of the next game, the serve passes to the receiver.

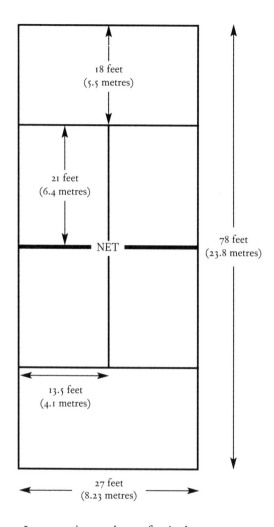

18 feet
(5.5 metres)

21 feet
(6.4 metres)

NET

78 feet
(23.8 metres)

13.5 feet
(4.1 metres)

27 feet
(8.23 metres)

Lawn tennis court layout for singles

The game is scored as follows: 'love' for no points (from the French word for egg, *l'oeuf*, symbolizing nothing); '15' for the first point; '30' for the second; '40' for the third; 'game' for the fourth. However, if both players have three points, i.e. it is 40–40, the score is called 'deuce' (from the old French *deus*, meaning two), and play continues until one or other of the players has achieved two clear points, known as advantages. If a player wins the first advantage but loses the second, so that his opponent equals once more, the score returns to deuce. The server's score is always called first, for example, if the server wins the first point, the score is 15–love; if he loses the next two points the score becomes 15–30. Six games must be won to win a set, and there are a maximum of five sets to be played in men's tennis, and three sets in women's tennis.

Players change ends after the first, third and every subsequent alternate game of each set, and at the end of each set, unless the total number of games in the set is even, in which case the change is not made until the end of the first game of the next set.

Tennis, as we know it today, has only been played since the 1870s. It is correctly referred to as lawn tennis. The general game of tennis, however, has been around for a long time. There were ball games in ancient times, and one theory is that tennis originated from a Roman game called 'harpastum', which was adapted in the Basque country, where it was known as *jeu do paume* as the ball was hit against a wall with the palm of the hand.

Popular thinking is that the first truly recognizable version of the game originated in France. In the eleventh century, a game of handball played over a rope and known as *jeu de paume* or *longue-paume*, was played in the cloisters of monasteries, and it became such a distraction from prayer that the pope banned it. Play continued in spite of this – the

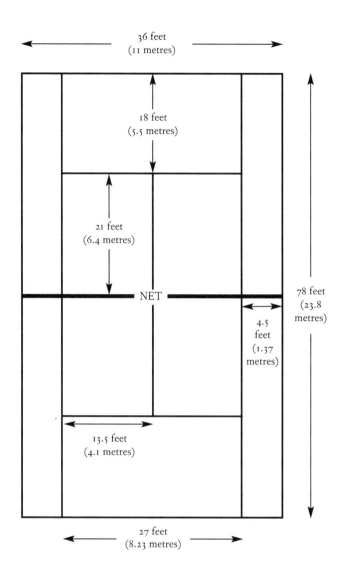

Lawn tennis court layout for doubles

quadrangle of the cloister grounds providing the perfect court, and with room for as many as six players on each side of the rope.

As the game evolved, players took to wearing toughened gloves in order to deliver a harder shot than that which was manageable with the bare hand, and some gloves even had strings across them. Meanwhile, other players began to make use of wooden bats. The racket is thought to be an Italian invention of the fourteenth century. By 1500, some rackets included strings across the head, probably made from the muscle tissue of the intestines of sheep. Interestingly, the guts of seven sheep are necessary to form the strings of one lawn tennis racket, and, for the record, catgut strings have nothing to do with cats. Rather 'cat' is a corruption of 'kit', a seventeenth-century violin, which probably had sheep-gut strings, hence the confusion. Synthetic strings have been used from the nineteenth century.

Early tennis balls were made of leather, stuffed with hair or wool. (In England, in the sixteenth century, it was quite common for people to sell their hair to stuff tennis balls.) With the invention of rackets, balls got harder and heavier; in fact some were quite dangerous, being hard enough to cause serious injury to a player.

The game's popularity spread from cloister to castle, and, by the fourteenth century, tennis was being played at Court. As a game played by the nobility, it now achieved a new sophistication, and this form of the game was known as 'court-paume'. Court-paume was played on indoor courts and had more complex rules than anything before it. The best of eleven games were played, with the winning side reaching

French tennis, 1632

six games first – perhaps the origin of today's six games wins a set.

There are several theories that early French tennis games were played to 60 points, rather than to today's 40 points. In France, in the early Middle Ages, sixty was a significant number, as one hundred is now, so it is possible that this would have been chosen as the winning score. Another speculation for the game being played to 60 points, however, is that the score was fixed around betting. Betting on games was very common (later, Henry VIII incurred financial problems due to his massive wagers on the tennis court), and it is possible that in medieval France the currency was divided into sixty units, which would be gambled fifteen at a time. This is supported by the fact that certain laws in the thirteenth and fourteenth centuries prohibited stakes higher than sixty deniers. A coin in circulation at this time was worth fifteen deniers, so perhaps a winning score was actually worth its equivalent in money, a theory that would mean that the scoring was once 15, 30, 45 and 60 points.

Another supposition is that in the court-paume game, a clock face would be used to record the score. Thus, when the first point was won, a quarter move of the appropriate hand was made, and so on, until a complete circuit had been made, which signified the end of a game.

By the late fourteenth century, tennis had reached England, and rapidly grew in popularity. Not everyone was keen on this turn of events, however. The public found church walls and their environs excellent playing areas, and it caused the authorities great consternation that this new ball game drew enthusiastic crowds to outside churches, but few as willingly inside. In the fifteenth century, the authorities at Exeter Cathedral declared themselves alarmed by the distractions of 'tenys' and, in 1469, the authorities at Tewkesbury Abbey were much put out when a large crowd gathered outside the abbey gates to watch a game being played there. Yet, church leaders and the monasteries enjoyed sporting privileges themselves, including ball games. What they feared most was loss of control.

Previously, under the feudal system, there had been little time for sporting play, and, while a certain amount of frivolity was tolerated among the general populace to keep them content and thus out of mischief, many churchmen and governors were anxious that in games lay the seeds of anarchy and vice. Now that the masses were showing such fondness for sporting pastimes, they were concerned. In 1462, the Manorial Court at Sherborne in Dorset forbade the playing of tennis under pain of both fine and imprisonment, while tennis was also one of a long list of games banned by the Borough Ordinances of Leicester in the fifteenth century. Sporting events that drew large crowds were considered a public nuisance, and the government was worried that 'frivolous' games were distracting the populace from more necessary sports, such as archery or, indeed, from work. Perhaps rightly so. In 1588, a French visitor was surprised to find Englishmen playing tennis on a working day, and for money.

As in France, tennis became popular with the Court, and thus 'real' or as it was originally called 'royal' tennis came into being. Played with rackets on indoor courts, it became exclusive from the less sophisticated handball game played by the general populace. Both Henry VII and Henry VIII were accomplished players. Henry VIII, reputedly champion of England, built the original real tennis court at Hampton Court Palace, and legend has it that he invented the term 'service'. Supposedly, when he grew too fat to throw his own ball in the air, he would shout 'service', at which cry a servant standing by would throw the ball for him.

In the sixteenth century there were apparently more than a thousand royal tennis courts in Paris alone. William Shakespeare famously wrote about the game in his play *Henry V*, in which France and England are preparing to do battle:

FIRST AMBASSADOR

> *He therefore sends you, meeter for your spirit,*
> *This tun of treasure; and, in lieu of this,*
> *Desires you let the dukedoms that you claim*
> *Hear no more of you. This the Dauphin speaks.*

KING HENRY

> *What treasure, uncle?*

EXETER

> *Tennis-balls, my liege.*

KING HENRY

> *We are glad the Dauphin is so pleasant with us;*
> *His present and your pains we thank you for:*
> *When we have match'd our rackets to these balls,*
> *We will, in France, by God's grace, play a set*
> *Shall strike his father's crown into the hazard.*
> *Tell him he hath made a match with such a wrangler*
> *That all the courts of France will be disturb'd*
> *With chaces.*

Charles I and II enjoyed the game. George IV was known to be a keen player, and Prince Albert owned a locker in the changing room at Hampton Court. Edward VII and George V were also participants in the game. Not for nothing then has real tennis been called the game of kings.

In spite of this, general interest in the game waned during the seventeenth century and play was virtually non-existent in France by 1800. In the mid-nineteenth century there was a revival of the game among the English upper classes and many courts were added to country estates, but by then a new game of tennis had emerged.

In the summer of 1859, a solicitor by the name of Major Harry Gem and merchant Mr J. B. Perera invented an outdoor version of tennis called 'lawn rackets' that was adapted for play on grass; in fact they played on the lawn of the latter's house in Edgbaston, Birmingham. In 1872, together with Dr Arthur Tomkins and Dr Frederick Haynes, they founded the Leamington Lawn Tennis Club – the world's first lawn tennis club.

Then, in 1874, Major Walter Clopton Wingfield, a retired army officer and gentleman farmer in Wales, patented an outdoor tennis game which he called by the Greek name 'Sphairistike', a name which thankfully he was persuaded to abandon. Except for the court – Sphairistike was meant to be played on a court shaped like an hourglass, widening out from the centre at each end – this new form of the game was the start of the tennis game we know today. Matches took place outdoors, on a court without walls, and the court was a grass one (real tennis games were played on a stone floor). Essentially, it was played with the new rubber-type ball, (later covered with cloth) which allowed for play on grass.

Lawn tennis caught the imagination of the upper and middle classes, and it was not long before courts were being added to gardens, and tennis parties added to summer socials. Private clubs were also opened countrywide. In 1877, the All-England Croquet Club at Wimbledon changed its name to The All England Croquet and Lawn Tennis Club (in 1882, 'Croquet' was dropped from the title, although it was reinstated in 1899, to the All England Lawn Tennis and Croquet Club). The first Wimbledon Lawn Tennis Championships was held that year, and, for this occasion, a new set of rules and scoring was adopted, which afterwards became standard for lawn tennis. Additionally, the court was changed to a rectangular one of

A game of Sphairistike

78 feet by 27 feet (23.8 metres by 8.23 metres). Twenty-one players competed, and, on 19 July, twenty-seven-year-old Spencer William Gore, from Wimbledon – a surveyor by trade, and also a keen cricketer – became the first lawn tennis champion, beating William Marshall to win the men's singles.

In 1888, the Lawn Tennis Association was founded and soon had representatives all over the British Isles. Thus the game became standardized nationwide. William Renshaw, who won Wimbledon six times, became the LTA's first president. By 1897, the LTA had sanctioned seventy-three tournaments, and, also in that year, forty-three new rules were introduced, few of which have changed significantly to this day. In the early 1900s, King George V became patron of the association.

Lawn tennis's popularity had also spread abroad, and international competition began. The first international contest was between the British Isles and the USA in 1883, and was held at the All England Club, Wimbledon. On this occasion it was victory to the British, but when the first Davis Cup tie (named after its founder, leading American player Dwight F. Davis) was played in 1900, the USA emerged triumphant. Men's singles and doubles were included in the Athens Olympic games of 1896, with J. P. Boland of Ireland and G. Traun of Germany taking gold medals.

[86]

Miss L. Dod, five-time Wimbledon champion

By 1906, the Wimbledon championship had become the most important worldwide event on the tennis calendar. The first meeting of the International Lawn Tennis Association was held in March 1913, with member countries being Great Britain, France, Australasia, Austria, Belgium, Denmark, Germany, Netherlands, Russia, South Africa, Spain, Sweden and Switzerland. The USA joined later in 1923.

By the end of the nineteenth century, women as well as men had achieved recognition as serious players. The Irish pioneered a women's championship as part of the inaugural Irish Championships of 1879, and its first female champion was fourteen-year-old May Langrishe. A mixed-doubles game was pioneered in the same year, and the first women's doubles championship was played at the Northern Lawn Tennis Championships in Manchester. The West of England Championships, held in Bath, also included a women's doubles that year. In 1884, Wimbledon staged a women's singles championship for the first time, and, in 1900, women's lawn tennis events were included in the Paris Olympics, with British player Charlotte Cooper becoming the first woman gold medallist. At first, women played in long skirts, but by the 1920s hemlines were rising to allow greater freedom of movement on the court. In 1923, the Wightman Cup, a competition for British and American women's teams, was first held. It was named after Hazel Hotchkiss Wightman, an American, and one of the most successful players in the years before and after the First World War. She donated the cup.

The 1920s and 1930s are regarded as the golden years of lawn tennis due to the many fine players they produced. It was in the 1920s that seeding was introduced, that is the placing of selected players in certain places in the draw to prevent them meeting each other until the later games. Also, from the 1920s onwards, professional players made money from one-off exhibition games, and, although the main tournaments remained amateur, leading players were paid unofficially for their performances. The distinction between professionals and amateurs in their competitions was dropped by the LTA in 1967. The International Tennis Federation approved open professionalism in 1968. In the first open Wimbledon of 1968, the men's prize money was £2,000 and the women's £750.

Tennis remains an extremely popular game worldwide.

According to the Lawn Tennis Association, 3.5 million people aged four years upwards played tennis in the United Kingdom alone in 2002.

MAZES

For those who like to lose themselves, or perhaps their guests, in the garden, and who have a fondness for a pair of shears, a puzzle hedge may be the ultimate garden entertainment.

As most gardens are unlikely to have a spare overgrown hedge that can be shaped into a maze, an alternative way of constructing a garden maze would be to plot a design using stones, pebbles, pieces of wood and lengths of string. Though perhaps not as exciting as weaving in and out of a dense hedgerow, it would nevertheless provide an entertaining diversion for children who are particularly keen on solving labyrinthian puzzles.

Mazes have been created since antiquity, although high hedge mazes did not appear until much later. Henry VIII built a multicursal puzzle maze with high hedges at Nonsuch Palace, of which Antony Watson wrote: 'You will enter a tortuous path and fall into the hazardous wiles of the labyrinth'. However, at this time most garden mazes (or mases) were still crafted from small box borders, often framing a knot garden, or were floral mazes, with intricate pathways designed around low-lying flowerbeds.

Multicursal maze

In the thirteenth century, medieval Christian pavement mazes were laid in the stone floors of French cathedrals and were supposed to represent the journeys of the Crusades, with Jerusalem often depicted at their centres. More than this, they represented the pilgrimage of the individual believer. The Christian maze symbolized the idea of being spiritually lost, and, after wandering in the wilderness, finding the true path to the afterlife. In essence then, such mazes were allegories for the journey through life to death, or from sin to salvation. Before this, turf mazes may have been associated with pagan rituals, or, as argued by some, to represent the journey travelled when new settlers established themselves in foreign lands.

The first hedge mazes appeared in France and Italy, and the designs and gardening techniques were imported to Britain. French shrub labyrinths were called 'Dédales' after

Medieval Christian labyrinth

the mythical Daedalus who, so legend has it, built the famous labyrinth in Crete.

As topiary became more sophisticated, grand houses across Europe sported a maze in their grounds. However, their emphasis had moved away from the pavement maze, being more to do with decoration and mastery of design, rather than spiritual redemption. As the association with mazes became more secular, statuary and fountains were added to them, and the high hedges became convenient for a little dalliance and flirtation while lost. Materials for the hedges varied, including box, privet, yew, holly and white-thorn, among others.

The Puritans associated mazes with frivolity and pagan ritual. Many formal gardens contained mazes before the Civil

Ancient maze

War, but no mazes now date back to before Cromwell's rule. However, although houses and their gardens were destroyed in the uprising, the destruction of many mazes lay in the whimsy of fashion.

In 1712, Joseph Addison wrote: 'I would rather look upon a tree in all its luxuriancy and diffusion of branches, than when it is thus cut and trimmed into a mathematical figure; and cannot but fancy that an orchard in flower looks infinitely more delightful than all the labyrinths of the most finished parterre.' His words carried weight and many mazes were pulled down to make way for new ideas in garden design.

Garden ideology often took against the artificial form of the maze, yet, just as one gardener of the day announced its doom, some landed knight commissioned a new one, with new and more intricate designs being explored – some hosts seemed very determined to keep their guests within the maze! Thus, where one maze was pulled down, another was often built.

In the late 1800s, and for much of the nineteenth century, mazes were a popular attraction at tea gardens and in public parks. Additionally, in the nineteenth century, the Industrial Revolution created new wealth, and new landowners were keen to display their success. Copying the aristocracy, many added mazes to their houses by way of ostentation. No longer were mazes the preserve of the titled classes.

Mazes were neglected or lost during the First and Second World Wars, when garden areas were turned over to the growing of food. However, recently there has been renewed interest in the maze, and more are being built worldwide than at any time in their history, with renewed interest in their symbolism and potential for design.

The puzzle maze at Hampton Court, which covers a quarter of an acre, is the oldest and most famous hedge maze in Britain. The present maze dates from 1690 when it was replanted, but the original design was thought to have been laid out in Elizabethan times. The way to its heart is to turn left on entering the maze, then right twice, and left four times, while to get out again one turns right four times and left twice. Alternatively, one can keep a hand on the left wall at all times, which will bring one to the centre and out again, although it will also take one down the false turns and dead ends. Its design has been copied many times and it is a tourist attraction in its own right, many thousands of people wandering its paths each year.

QUOIT TENNIS

THIS is a tennis-like game for those who do not have enough room for a full court, and was described in 1947 as being 'a first-class game and the exercise value is great'. The game is played by serving rope rings underarm over a piece of rope stretched across the lawn. The rings must be served flat and the catcher must receive them with one hand only and then return them with that same hand. The quoit must be returned immediately, in any fashion except overarm, although it must be thrown from the same position in the court at which the catcher received it, and must pass over the rope.

Scoring can follow the same rules as lawn tennis, but a simpler version involves playing to fifteen points. Similar to the scoring system in badminton, points can only be scored with serve, and so only the 'in' (serving) side can gain points, with play passing to the 'out' side if the rally is lost. Only one serve is allowed, unless the quoit touches the net, when it can be taken again.

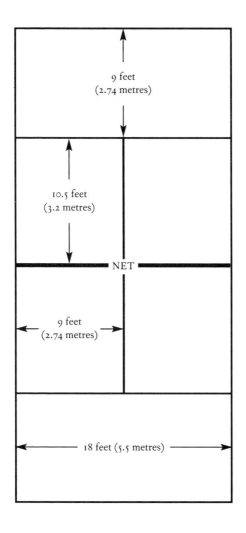

9 feet
(2.74 metres)

10.5 feet
(3.2 metres)

NET

9 feet
(2.74 metres)

18 feet (5.5 metres)

Quoit tennis court

ROUNDERS

A SUNNY summer's day is a good excuse for retrieving the rounders bats from the back of the garden shed. A ball, four posts, and some willing friends to field and bat, is then all that is needed to play. Rounders is actually an old English game, thought to have been played first in Tudor times. Fundamentally, it involves hitting a ball with a bat and, while the ball is being retrieved, making a dash round four posts to home.

The first written reference to the game dates from 1744, when 'baseball' was described in a publication called *A Little Pretty Pocketbook*. From the description, the game appears to be rounders rather than the popular American game, which is thought to have its origins in rounders anyway – although not all baseball fans accept this, however. By 1828, rounders was definitely called rounders, for *The Boy's Own Book* devoted a whole chapter to it.

To play at home, one will need a larger playing area than for other games. Rather more important than the size of the rounders field, is that the area chosen should be far enough away from the house or neighbouring houses to ensure that a hard-hitting batsman does not do damage to any windows, sunbathers, babies in prams or the like. It is worth remembering that bowlers can bowl at over 60 mph (97 kph), and some batters can hit the ball at even greater speeds.

Flowerbeds and shrubbery also need to be taken into account. On the bright side, they will make the fielders' job a greater challenge, and while the fielders are hard at work retrieving balls from beneath the rhododendrons, rounders may be scored.

Rounders players use truncheon-shaped bats and a leather-cased hard ball, similar in size to a tennis ball (in fact, a tennis ball will suffice for play at home), and is played on a 'field' marked up in an elongated diamond. At each corner of the diamond there is a 'post' or base. The home base is at one end, and first, second and third posts at the other points. Fourth post is situated along the line of third post toward home.

In the centre of the field is a square in which the bowler stands, facing the batsman. Directly behind the batsman is the backstop, while a baseman is placed at each post, and three fielders stand ready to catch or chase after the ball. Games are played between two teams, and, according to the rules, only nine players may be on the field at one time. Teams may have as many as fifteen players, however, or as few as six. Two innings are usually played in official matches.

To play, the bowler stands with both feet in the square and tosses the ball to the batsman. His bowl must be a smooth,

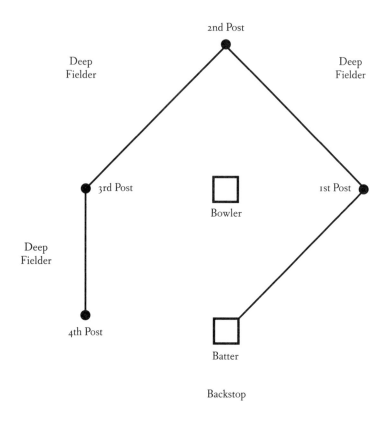

Plan of rounders field

underarm action that is below the head and above the knee, but not straight at the body. The ball must neither bounce, nor go wide. A 'no-ball' is called if the bowler does not bowl within these rules. The batter can run on a no-ball if he or she wishes, but once first post is reached, cannot change the decision to run. Note that two consecutive bad balls scores half a rounder for the batsman, without him even having to move.

Even in a garden game, it helps if someone neutral can be persuaded to act as umpire, and to decide when a no-ball situation has occurred. In serious rounders, usually two umpires preside over the match.

The batter must stand with both feet in the batting square. If either foot strays from the square before the batter hits or misses a good ball, he or she is out. If the ball is good, the batsman must attempt to hit it. He or she then makes a dash for first post, taking the bat with them. It should be noted that, unless obstructed, the batter is not allowed to run inside the posts, otherwise he or she will be given out.

If the ball is caught before it lands, the batter is out; similarly, if the fielders retrieve the ball quickly and stump first post before the batter gets to it, he or she is out. However, if the hit is a good one and has travelled far, the batter should aim to cover all the posts and get home, at which point – as long as he or she touches fourth post – a rounder is scored. A batter cannot be caught out off a no-ball, so if a no-ball is hit directly to a fielder in the outfield, for example, the batter can still run on a no-ball, and even score a rounder if he or she runs fast enough. If the ball is a backward hit, the batter can

Rounders bat and ball

only run as far as first post while the ball is in the backward area, but it is still possible to score a full rounder in these circumstances. If the batter fails to hit the ball, but still gets round the course before the next ball is bowled, a half rounder is scored. A half rounder is also scored if the batter reaches second post after hitting the ball, or if a fielder obstructs someone running round the course (the penalty is awarded to that player).

Fielders stop play by stumping (touching the ball to) the posts towards which a batsman is running, or by returning the ball to the bowler in the bowling square. Throwing the ball at a player is not allowed; although it was once, this was eliminated when the first official rounders rules were drawn up. If a batsman decides it is safer to stop at a post, rather than to risk running on to the next, he must maintain contact with that post, using his hand or bat, for as long as the bowler has possession of the ball within the bowling square. Otherwise the fielding team may stump the next post and he or she will be out. The batter cannot move on to further posts until the next ball has been bowled, but may start running as soon as the ball leaves the bowler's hand. There is no obligation to run on every ball, unless a player is following on one's heels. It is not permissible for two batters to be at the same post, and if this situation occurs, the first must run on, despite the risk of being run out.

The batter must also stop running when the bowler has the ball in the bowling square, but can run on to the next post if half-way between posts when the bowler catches the ball. While running, one must not overtake another player. Neither must one obstruct the fielders. Both of these are considered offences for which a player is out.

Oddly, although rounders originated in Tudor times, it did not become popular until about 1800. Even then, it was not an established game, and it was not until 1889 that it enjoyed serious interest. Around this time, two governing bodies were formed in England and Scotland – the National Rounders Association of Liverpool and surrounding areas, and the Scottish Rounders Association. The National Rounders Association was formed in 1943 to promote the best interests of the game. The first national tournament was held in Rhyl in 1976.

Although rounders has a reputation for being played in parks and gardens, on beaches, during picnics, and in schools, in fact it is played seriously all over Britain, and the National Rounders Association also promotes the game abroad.

SKITTLES

S KITTLES is a game with which everyone can have fun –
from dedicated bowlers to small children. A garden set
usually comprises nine bottle-shaped, wooden skittles, which
are arranged in a triangle or square shape, and small wooden
balls with which to knock them down.

Currently, the most commonly played skittles game in
England is known as West Country Skittles.

A total of nine skittles, with a height of 10 inches (25.4
centimetres) and a midway diameter of 4 inches (10.2 centimetres) are normally used in play. A 'kingpin', which is a pin
that is slightly larger than the others, may also be included
with the eight other skittles, and positioned at the front of the
skittles formation or in the middle. The ball used to knock

over the skittles is usually wooden, with an average diameter of 5 inches (12.7 centimetres).

Traditionally, the bowling area or 'alley' is made of wood, but skittles can also be played directly on grass. When marking out the alley on grass, it should have a width of 6 feet (1.8 metres), while the recommended distance from the throwing line to the front skittle is 24 feet (7.3 metres).

Before the wooden ball is thrown, the nine skittles must be arranged in a diamond shape at the far end of the alley, ensuring that the sides of the formation are diagonal to the straight edges of the alley markings. When each of the nine skittles are standing upright within the formation, with equal space between each skittle on either side, the first ball can be rolled.

Each turn consists of three throws, though it is important to remember that the ball must be rolled down the alley and not thrown. If all the skittles are knocked down on the first or second throw – called a 'sticker' – all the skittles are set up again in the correct formation. Any player achieving this feat would gain the maximum score per turn of twenty-seven points. If a kingpin has been used within the formation, a player can only score points if the kingpin has been knocked down, regardless of how many other skittles have been felled.

In a typical game of West Country skittles, two teams play a series of legs against each other, in which each leg consists of a single turn comprising three throws. The total number of points scored by each team player is added up and the team with the highest score wins the leg. The total number of legs per match can vary, but in certain areas, the first team to win five legs is usually declared the overall winner.

Skittles may be traced back to bowling-type games of 7,000 years ago, and although it is hard to prove that these are the specific ancestors of skittles, in 5,200 BC, the British Egyptologist, Sir Flinders Petrie, discovered a game that was notably similar in the tomb of an Egyptian child – both as a board game and an outdoor bowling game. Interestingly, the ancient Polynesians played a game called 'Ula Maika' in which stones were bowled at a target over a distance of 60 feet (18 metres) – the same as in tenpin bowling today.

In Germany, in the third and fourth centuries, monks played a game with their kegels – clubs that they carried for protection. The kegels were stood against a wall and the monks threw stones at them until they fell over. The game had the backing of the monasteries as the clubs were supposed to represent sin or temptation. A very similar game known as 'Knock-the-devil-down' was played in medieval England, and today the modern skittles game in Germany is called *kegelen*.

In the fourteenth century a game called 'club kayles' was played, which involved throwing clubs at skittles, rather than the clubs themselves being the target. This game included one skittle that was bigger than the others, and was positioned so as to be the hardest to knock down. The name 'kayles' or 'kails' is thought to derive from the French word *quilles*, which at some point changed to 'skittles'. An alternative derivation is from the Old Norse 'shuttle' referring to the ball or projectile thrown by the players. In Danish the word *skyttel* denotes a shuttle or marble.

In Britain, the modern game of skittles owes its existence to the good old British pub. Bowling alleys first came to London in 1455, and were extremely popular. The game of bowling at pins emerged, with the pins or skittles being positioned at the end of a lane or bowling alley. It is thought that the lanes were originally made of clay, and that, later, boards were placed on these.

There were many regional variations of the game, with differences in rules, alley length (in West Country skittles today, the alley is around 24 feet (7.3 metres) long, while in the game of 'Long Alley', played in the East Midlands, it is 33–36 feet (10–11 metres) in length), and the size, shape and number of the skittles. There could be between nine and fifteen pins, for example, and these could be arranged in a diamond, square or triangle formation.

Coloured pins were also used, supposedly to represent members of the royal court, and each had a different value, with the kingpin having the highest. Some games involved throwing balls, which differed in size and weight, and others the throwing of cheeses! In skittles terms, a 'cheese' is a lump suitable for throwing.

In 1469, it was documented that a large crowd gathered to watch skittling on the new bowling green outside Tewkesbury Abbey. A century later, in 1530, Henry VIII had bowling alleys added to his residence at Whitehall, and he not only enjoyed the game, but wagered heavily on it too.

As with other sports, gambling and the association with alehouses often brought the game into ill repute, and caused anxiety in those concerned with the public good. In America, in the early 1800s, ninepins was so popular, and gambling on it so rife, that it was banned. However, as only the game of ninepins had been outlawed and not bowling in general, in 1842 another pin was added, which solved the problem. Hence

the game of ten-pin bowling came to be played.

A London game called 'Old English Skittles' was once very popular in the pubs alongside the river Thames. The game was formalized in the nineteenth century with an Amateur Skittles Association being formed. It reached its height of popularity between the First and Second World Wars, when many competitions were held, but is rarely played today. However, other forms of alley skittles and ninepins are still regular pursuits.

SWINGBALL

I F there is no room for a tennis court in one's garden, swingball is a popular alternative for a tennis-type game. There is a theory that the idea for the modern game rests with Roman gladiators. Supposedly, a popular, and grisly, pastime in ancient Rome involved a poor unfortunate turning round in ever-faster circles, while swinging a ball and chain. A pair of combatants, meanwhile, took turns at swiping the ball with clubs, and no doubt there was carnage all round.

It does seem rather far-fetched to link this with the modern game. Certainly swingball today is not so savage – unless one has the misfortune to get in the way of one's opponent's bat, the rackets being quite thick and made of heavy-duty plastic.

Swingball can be played alone or against opponents. It involves hitting a tennis ball on the end of a rope that is attached to a steel pole. The pole is sunk securely into the ground, usually with the help of a metal pin. A spiral device at the top of the pole, and a nylon spring ring, which is attached to the rope and fastens on to the spiral, allows the rope to spin round the pole, but not to twist around it.

If there are two players, the rope will be in the middle of the spiral at the beginning of the game. To start the game, the

players toss for the first serve, and the server gets to choose whether he will serve clockwise or anti-clockwise, which he must stick to for the duration of the game. The server can also choose to serve from any spot around the pole, probably the one that avoids the willow tree or the sun's glare. When both players are ready, the server hits the ball round the pole to the receiver. Players hit the ball alternately. According to which player is the stronger, the rope will move to the top or to the bottom of the pole. A game is completed when the spring ring reaches the end of the spiral – top or bottom. If the players are evenly matched, some quite energetic rallies can be played, and of course there is the advantage that one doesn't have to lose time in retrieving the ball. Players take it in turns to serve at the end of each game, and each time the server may choose the direction in which he or she wishes to play.

There is also a doubles version of the game, although it is not worth hunting in the swingball box for more rackets, as each pair plays with one between them, exchanging the racket between shots. The pairs take up positions on opposite sides of the pole, and play follows the rules of the singles game.

Interestingly, while swingball appears to be well known in English-speaking countries, it is hardly played in continental Europe.

TUG OF WAR

Tʜɪs is an ancient game that has its origins in primitive times. In early Christianity the game was thought to be encouraged by the Church to represent the struggle between good and evil. 'Tug o' war' was often played on Shrove Tuesday, supposedly to purge baser energies in preparation for Lent.

To play this one needs a strong, sturdy rope and two teams of several people, who pull against each other at either end of the rope. A team is declared the winner when either the opposing team collapses or when a scarf or similar marker in the centre of the rope crosses a marked line, usually because one team has used their superior strength to pull their opponents across the line.

In medieval times, people liked to indulge in a little horseplay. Here the game was played with a belt or leather strap, with three people at either end of it – one acting as the head of an animal, one as the body, and one riding it. The object of the game was naturally to unseat the other team's rider.

VOLLEYBALL

———————————

B Y making use of a badminton net already positioned across a lawn, one can have additional fun in the garden with a game of volleyball. Although there are official measurements for the size of the court, one can adapt these as necessary for an informal game to fit the garden space available.

Volleyball is a team game played by two teams on a playing court divided by a net. Teams can be single sex or mixed, with either two, three, four or six players in a team on court at any one time. The game can be played indoors on a court or outside, either on a grassy space or on a beach.

The ball, made of either flexible leather or a synthetic equivalent, with a rubber or rubber-like inner, must have a circumference of 25.5–26 inches (65–67 centimetres), and weigh between 10–10.5 ounces (260–280 grams). Playing areas vary according to the volleyball code observed, but the courts are approximately 60 feet (18 metres) long by 30 feet (9 metres) wide with a centre line. Official net height is 7.97 feet (2.43 metres), but is reduced to 6.89 feet (2.1 metres) for children under thirteen years old, and 7.35 feet (2.24 metres) for under sixteens and all women competitors. The height of the net in a garden game of volleyball will therefore vary according to the age and gender of the players.

In outdoor volleyball the court may be marked out by a rope, and if that rope should be disturbed during a rally, players and referees must imagine where the rope should be positioned and play accordingly for the rest of the rally.

The object of the game is for each team to hit the ball regularly over the net, using hands and arms only, and to ground the ball in their opponent's court while simultaneously preventing their opponents from doing the same. A ball is put into play when the right back-row player serves by hitting the ball over the net. A rally often ensues with each team allowed to hit the ball on their side of the net a maximum of three times each turn, including the shot returning the ball to their opponents' side. A 'block' contact is allowed in addition to these three hits, which is when the receiver parries a ball that has been returned with great speed. With the exception of the block, no player is allowed to hit the ball twice consecutively. A rally continues until the ball is either grounded in play, hit out of play, or if one team fails to return the ball or commits a fault or foul.

With six-a-side volleyball, the team players must adopt a particular team formation, and keep to this formation

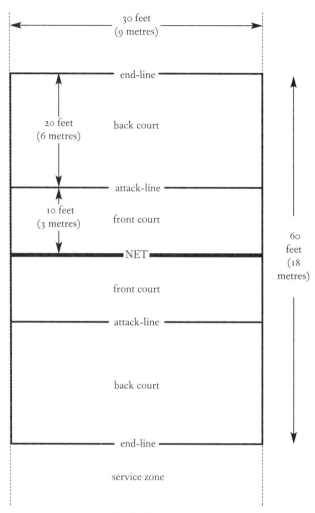

Volleyball court

throughout the match, moving round one position clockwise when serving. When the opposing team is serving, the receiving team does not rotate, and stays in the same position.

Serve rotates through the team in strict order, with each member taking a turn. When serving, the ball is tossed up about a metre into the air and then struck with the hand or any part of the arm. The ball may be hit with the hand in a number of ways and the different shots have evocative names. The 'roll shot' is where the ball is hit with the heel or palm of the hand, but a player may also choose a 'cobra', using straight, locked fingertips, or a 'camel toe' where the fingers are knurled. The ball may also be played with the back of the hand from the wrist to the knuckles. An ace is a point-winning service that is achieved when the receiver is unable to reach the ball or keep it in play

A ball may touch the net at any time without penalty, other than during service when this constitutes a fault, with serve then passing to the opposition. A ball driven into the net, but which is still in play, may be recovered within the limit of the three permissible team contacts. If two players from opposing side make contact with the ball simultaneously over the net, the ball remains in play and the receiving team is allowed another three hits.

The block shot is crucial and occurs during defensive play of a hard driven ball. The ball may be momentarily lifted or pushed provided this is executed in one continuous motion. A ball may also be 'set' by one player, where two hands are used to direct the ball into the perfect position for another player to strike it. In the case of both the block and the set shot the action must be continuous and no attempt to hold the ball is allowed.

During any game each side is allowed a maximum of two time-outs per set lasting a maximum of thirty seconds. In games of two or three per side no substitutions are allowed,

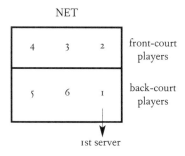

NET

| 4 | 3 | 2 | front-court players |
| 5 | 6 | 1 | back-court players |

1st server

Rotational player positions

though, infinite substitutions are permissible in the four or six-a-side game.

Matches can comprise either the best of three sets or the best of five. Teams must score a minimum of 15 points to win a set, but must also win by a margin of two points. For example, if the score is 14–14, play continues until 16–14 or 17–15. However, if the set is still tied at 16–16, the first team to score the next point to reach 17 becomes the set winner. In a three-set match the first two sets are won with 15 points and a winning margin of two points, as above, but the final set is won by the first team to score 7 points, there being no necessary winning margin. Points are only scored with serve, similar to the scoring system used in badminton. If a rally is lost then the serve changes sides. However, in the deciding set, points are won according to which team wins the rally, like tennis, and is not dependent upon which team is serving.

The game of volleyball was invented in 1895 at the Young Men's Christian Association (YMCA) in Holyoke, Massachusetts, by William G. Morgan, the son of a Welsh immigrant and a YMCA Director of Education. He had been motivated to create a simple game that was less physical than basketball, and suitable for people of a wide range of different physiques. Drawing on aspects of basketball, baseball and tennis, he designed 'mintonette'. In this new game, a tennis net was raised to a level of about 6.5 feet (2 metres), just a few inches above average head height, and players played a hand-ball game across it, volleying the ball back and forth. During a demonstration of the game, it was pointed out that 'volleyball' would be a more apt name, and 'mintonette' was soon dropped in favour of 'volleyball' at the 1896 YMCA Conference.

The first game of volleyball was played at Springfield College on 7 July 1896, and the sport quickly caught on. Initially, a team comprised of nine players in three rows of three, with regular rotations ensuring that every team member had a turn in every court position during the game. Later, the net height increased to 7.5 feet (2.3 metres), and the number of players per team was reduced to six. A lighter leather ball was specially created for the game in 1900. By 1907, volleyball was presented at the Playground of America convention as one of the country's most popular sports.

Volleyball was introduced into Western Europe in 1918 by US servicemen at the end of the First World War, indeed, a year later American Expeditionary Forces distributed 16,000 volleyballs to its troops and allies. By 1919 the game had been introduced into Britain. Due mostly to the support and promotion of the YMCA movement, volleyball was growing in popularity throughout the world; in North America, Europe, the East and in the Southern Hemisphere. Though it had begun life as a mere leisure activity, volleyball was becoming one of the world's most popular competitive sports.

By the 1920s, various rules and styles of play had been established, and in 1928, the United States Volleyball Association (now known as USA Volleyball), was formed to set up tournaments and standardize the rules of the game, and the first US Open was held. Eight years later, at the Berlin Olympics, discussions were held by representatives of twenty-two countries about the possibility of organizing volleyball on an international level, and in 1939, at the World University Games, the first international volleyball tournament took place. After the Second World War, in April 1947, the International Volleyball Federation was formed, and two years later, the first world championships for men were held in Prague, followed by the first women's world championships in 1952. By the early 1950s it was estimated that over 50 million people were playing volleyball in over sixty countries.

In 1964, volleyball was played at the Olympics in Tokyo for the first time, becoming the first Olympic team sport for both men and women. The beach volleyball game, which had appeared in the 1920s and 1930s, was also made an Olympic sport, but not until 1996 in Atlanta.

Today, volleyball's popularity remains undiminished, with 800 million players around the world playing the game at least once a week, whether it be on an indoor court, on a beach or in the garden.

CHILDREN'S
GAMES

MANY traditional children's games have survived to this day, and there is much fun to be had playing them. Here follows a small selection perfect for children and grown-ups too.

BALL GAMES

Note: for the following three games, its is better to use a soft sponge ball or a tennis ball.

Ball game in Roman Britain

BAD EGGS

For this game several players are needed. One player throws a ball into the air, and, while it is ascending, the others run as far away as they can. The 'chaser' catches the ball and yells 'Stop!' On hearing this call the other players must now stand still. The chaser then aims the ball at a player of their choice, probably the easiest one to hit, or perhaps the one that they particularly wish to eliminate from the game. If the selected target is hit, the chaser calls, 'Bad Egg!' and the player is out of the game. The game continues until all players have been hit. The last one in then becomes the chaser.

PIGGY IN THE MIDDLE

THREE players are needed for this game. Players stand in a line so that one is in the middle of the other two. The two players on the outside then proceed to throw a ball to each other over the head of the player in the middle. Play continues until the player in the middle intercepts the ball, at which point he or she changes places with the person who last threw the ball.

STATUES

THE player holding the ball stands in the middle of the other players, who form a circle. The thrower then tosses the ball to any person at random. Should a player miss the ball, they must remain frozen in stance – no matter how awkward the pose – until the end of the game. The last person to receive the ball when all the other players are frozen is the winner, and he or she will replace the person standing in the middle of the circle.

BLIND MAN'S
BUFF

T HIS ancient game may have its roots in some form of
tribal rite. It is still played in many parts of the world
today. To play, one person stands in the centre of a circle and
is blindfolded. He or she is then spun round by the other
players; in some versions, a rhyme is chanted while this
occurs. After the blindfolded player has finished spinning, the

other participants scatter around the circle and stand still, while the disorientated person wearing the blindfold, the 'blind man', tries to catch them. The first player to be caught receives a 'buff', which in Middle English meant a 'blow', and whose usage in this sense is now unique to the game. The 'blow' in days gone by would not have been heavy, and certainly in the modern version of this game, a light touch will suffice. The first player to be touched becomes the next catcher.

An extended version of the game involves the 'blind man' having to feel the face of the person caught, who must then be identified correctly for the game to end.

FOLLOW THE LEADER

A GAME that will probably involve zigzagging in and out of the rosebushes, and ducking and diving under other obstacles, Follow the Leader is a pastime of very long standing, and any number of people can join in. The rules are simple: the person at the front is 'the leader', behind whom the rest of the players form a queue. The leader then begins to move – and so does everyone else! From that point onwards, everyone copies the leader's every move and action, and any person failing to do so must drop out of line. The last person left behind the leader takes his place for the next round.

HIDE AND SEEK

ONE child is chosen to be the seeker and, with eyes closed, counts to an agreed number – up to fifty or one hundred – while the other players run and hide. When the count is up, the seeker shouts, 'Coming, ready or not!' and starts to search for the hideaways. The first person to be found is the new seeker, but all players must be found before the new seeker takes his turn.

A variation on the game is that the spot where the seeker stands and counts is called 'home'. The other players must then attempt to come out of hiding at a point when the seeker is away from 'home' and race back to the spot. If the player achieves this, they are still in the game. However, if the seeker manages to catch them before they reach 'home', the player is out.

HOOPS

THE game of hoops was probably invented along with the wheel. Originally, players propelled their hoops (often barrel hoops) along the length of a designated course, the winner being the first to cross the finish line. Traditionally, hoops were propelled with an implement such as a small stick, and only this could touch the hoop – using one's hand to guide its path ensured disqualification.

In the 1960s the plastic Hula Hoop was invented, whose lighter weight made them more ideal for spinning round one's waist or arm, or throwing in the air, than for racing.

HOPSCOTCH

ALTHOUGH this classic game is now thought of as a child's pastime, hopscotch originated with the Roman army, who used it both as a recreation and as a training exercise to improve their performance on the battlefield. As well as the ability to hop and jump, the game requires a high degree of agility and balance, and faultless footwork, which is perhaps why few adults play the game today.

Hopscotch was introduced to ancient Britain during the early Roman Empire. The original hopscotch courts were

more than 100 feet (30 metres) long, and foot soldiers completed the course in full armour. It is said that the courts were supposed to represent the Great North Road, the 400-mile Roman road from Glasgow to London, which was frequently used by the army.

Children imitated the soldiers, marking out their own courts, and, at some point, a scoring system was introduced. Varying forms of the game were known throughout Europe; it is called *marelles* in France, *templehupfen* in Germany, and *Hinkelbaan* in the Netherlands.

To play the game at home, a court somewhere in the region of 4 feet (1.2 metres) wide and 10 feet (3.1 metres) long must be chalked up on an appropriate site, such as an even patio or paved terrace. Court designs vary, but most are grid-like, consisting of a series of squares, some double and some single. The square in the middle will usually be split into four triangles, marking areas where both feet may be put down at once. At the top of the court, a semi-circle should be drawn, and this should be given an appropriate name, such as 'home', 'heaven' or 'out', to signify the end of the course. In Victorian times, 'plum pudding' was a popular choice, signifying an imaginary reward for the winner.

Once the court is finished, each player should find a marker, known as a puck – a few garden stones will be sufficient. The players take it in turns to throw, or rather to 'pink' their marker to the end of the course, aiming for the semi-circle marked as 'home', or whatever has been chosen. The player who lodges his marker there begins play.

The rules of hopscotch are many and various. One version of the game is as follows. Player one tosses his or her marker

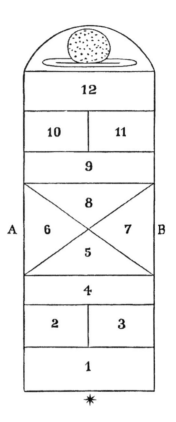

One of many possible hopscotch court designs

into the first square. The marker must land within the square – if it is touching a line it does not qualify, and the player forfeits a turn. If successful, the player hops into the square and then hops and jumps their way through the court, with the left foot landing in any left square and the right foot in any of the right ones. Single squares must be hopped into on one foot, using alternate feet.

Should the player step on a line, miss a square, or put a

foot down inappropriately, his turn ends and he goes back to square one. However, to allow the player a little leeway, some squares can be designated safe areas, and may be marked 'neutral', 'rest', or such like, and may be hopped through, as the player prefers.

When the player reaches the end of the court, they turn around and hop back in reverse order. If this is done without error, they then toss their marker into square two and begin again. The winner is the first player to complete the course for every numbered square on the court.

There are innumerable additional rules to complicate what most people think of as a simple game. Some players prefer to throw the marker before every move on the court, for example, rather than at the start of a round. Courts can also be drawn up as circles or spirals.

It must be said that hopscotch is not the easiest of games for the unpractised, but given a little time and energy it can be enormous fun.

JACKS

Most people will have owned a set of jacks at some point in their childhood. The word 'jack' was used to describe objects smaller than the ordinary, so perhaps this is why the game is so called. In a game of jacks, ten small, six-pronged metal objects with bobbles on the end, which look like three-dimensional crosses, are laid on the ground. A small ball, somewhat bigger than the jacks, is then bounced in the air. While the ball remains in the air, the player picks up as many jacks as possible before catching the ball. He may keep the jacks until the end of the game. If he fails to catch the ball, however, he must put the jacks back. The winner is the player in possession of the most jacks.

There are variations on the game; 'fivestones', for example, is played with five jacks, or five stones if preferred, and players have to pick up first one jack for one throw of the ball, then two, and then three, building up to picking up all five.

Historically, jacks is one of the oldest and most widely played games in the world and has been played with beans, stones and even bones. Children in ancient Egypt played with sheep knucklebones, the origin of the game 'knucklebones', which later became 'jacks'. At one time, jacks was played with a wooden ball, but with the invention of vulcanized rubber in the nineteenth century, the rubber bouncing ball took its place. It was sometimes played to the accompaniment of counting songs, such as, 'This Old Man', with the words '. . . he played one', '. . . he played two', corresponding to the number of jacks collected.

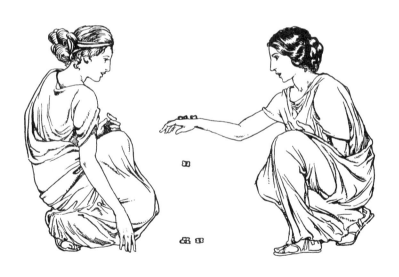

Girls playing the ancient Roman version of knuckle-bones

MARBLES

Mᴀʀʙʟᴇs is a popular children's pastime, commonly played with small, glass balls. Adults of today will no doubt have fond memories of their collection of 'aggies', 'alleys' and 'cat-eyes'. Indeed the envy of one's friends' marbles, the desire to win them, and the fear of losing one's own favourites – to say nothing of the pocket money they cost – can never be forgotten.

There are many games one can play with a bag of marbles, including those where marbles are aimed at holes, at arches or at a target. However, it can be argued that some of these are variations of the same game.

One of the best known games is 'Ring Taw', which is played on a smooth surface, upon which a circle of about 18 inches (45.7 centimetres) in diameter is mapped out with chalk or tape. In the garden, the patio might be the most suitable place to play; alternatively, a dusty corner, where the ground is dry and flat is ideal, and the circle can be drawn with a stick. All the marbles are put together into the centre of the circle and a larger one, known as the shooter or 'taw', is used to knock them out of the ring. Ideally, one wants to knock one's opponent's marbles out of the ring, which one then gets to keep – 'keepsies'. It should always be decided before a game starts whether one is 'playing for keeps', that is, keeping all the marbles one wins, or 'playing for fair', that is, returning all marbles to their rightful owner at the end of the game. A player may continue to shoot until he fails to get a marble out. It is then someone else's go. If the first player has failed to knock a marble out, but has left his shooter in the ring, his shooter may also be shot at by the following player. Rules should also be agreed upon in what is to be done in this situation. In some games, singles, for example, play may end if a player's taw is taken, unless he or she has a small arsenal of shooters. Quite often, an ordinary marble is given in exchange for the shooter, so that play can continue. In some more punitive games, a player's entire winnings must be handed over in return for the shooter. Needless to say, many rules are made up as play progresses.

However, it is not just children who 'knuckle down' in a marbles game, for it is a pastime that is enjoyed by adults too. A formal version of Ring Taw is played as an adult pub game, and players show off their skills in an annual World Marbles Championship, held on Good Friday at Tinsley Green, West Sussex. The game is similar to the one outlined above, but is played within a ring of 6 feet (1.83 metres) in diameter and forty-nine marbles are used, with the larger marble being called the 'tolley'. It can be played as a singles game, but in official games two teams of six members challenge each other. To ensure that there are no doubts about which marbles have been knocked out of play, in official contests, the game is played on a raised stone. Shots must be taken with a knuckle on the ring surface. The winning team is the one that collects the most marbles.

Traditionally, the time between Ash Wednesday and Good Friday is when marbles is played in Britain. (Eastertide was traditionally associated with outdoor revelry, when people relaxed from the restraints and denials of Lent. Whereas people of today might indulge in an excess of chocolate eggs, our ancestors took to the green.)

For at least the last three hundred years, a marble tournament has been played at Tinsley Green. Local legend has it that, in the time of Elizabeth I, two men were fighting for the love of a lady, and the suitors finally settled the matter by challenging each other to a game of marbles.

People have been playing marbles for centuries. The earliest marbles were made of flint, stone, bone, nuts or baked clay. They have been found in ancient Egyptian tombs and archaeologists have also found marbles in Mexico that date back to

100 BC. Clay marbles were popular in Roman times, and, as far as we know, marbles of one type or another – even ones made of real marble – have been played with in Europe ever since. In 1560, Brueghel painted children playing marbles, while in the eighteenth century, the poet and artist William Blake painted an illustration of three boys playing with marbles to illustrate his poem 'The Schoolboy'.

In Renaissance Italy, glass marbles began to be made in Venice, and, around 1800, china marbles also appeared. However, these were much too expensive to be used in a game by ordinary folk, who probably made do with common stones. Then, in 1846, a German glassblower invented a tool called the marble scissors. Although the marbles were still handcrafted, the 'scissors' made production fast enough to bring down marble prices, so that, for the first time, the public could afford them. From about 1860 to 1920 there was a thriving trade in German marbles, which were beautiful to look at, and were popular throughout Europe and America. There is now a large collector's market for them.

Modern glass marbles appear to have been introduced in America in about 1860 and until the Great Depression marble makers competed with each other to produce the most unique designs. Clay marbles were also being produced in large numbers in both Europe and America.

By the early years of the twentieth century machines were being used to produce perfectly round glass marbles, which improved the game. When the First World War cut off supplies of the German marbles to America, marbles began to be mass-produced there, and, until the Second World War, America became the dominant marble maker. After this, 'cats-eyes' from Japan became very popular, and, by the 1960s, nearly all marbles were being produced in the Far East. However, in the 1970s marble-making shifted again, this time to Mexico.

Obviously a market for marbles still exists, but the game's popularity has dipped in recent years, as computer games and multimedia products have driven children indoors. Nevertheless, various expressions associated with the game are still common parlance – 'playing for keeps', 'knuckling down' and, of course, 'to lose one's marbles'.

SKIPPING

KIPPING has kept many a lone child amused, and it is also a great form of exercise. Any adult who has recently tried to skip over a rope while counting in time will probably be puffing and panting by a count of thirty, whereas children think nothing of trying for a count of one hundred, and starting over again each time they achieve or fail to reach a target. Single rope skipping can be done on the spot, or running about if the skipper can do so without tripping.

Skipping games usually involve three or more children. Two children each hold one end of a length of rope and begin to turn the rope so that it just touches the ground in the middle. A third person then runs in to jump over the rope as it turns. If their feet make contact with the rope it will stop turning and they will have to try again. Two players can jump at once if the rope is long enough, or sometimes many people run in and out, taking it in turns to jump the rope. It is better if the rope is thrown backwards over the head, rather than forward under the feet.

'Double Dutch' skipping is an alternative type of skipping, which involves the use of two ropes turning in opposite directions.

Historians believe that the practice of skipping originated with the ropemakers of ancient Egypt or China. These skilled workers had to twist long strands of hemp to make the ropes, and they would jump over the rope in progress as they bent to pick up another strand. They became very adept at this, and it is thought that children imitated them. Travellers spread the game, and it has been enjoyed by children ever since.

Increasingly, adults are being encouraged to take up the pastime, and it is certainly a cheap, simple and quick way to get in shape for summer.

PUB
GARDEN
GAMES

AUNT SALLY

A UNT SALLY is a simple pastime in theory, the object of the game being to knock a wooden skittle (known as the doll or dolly) off the top of a 4-foot (1.2-metre) high metal post (the iron) by throwing sticks at it. However, in practice, participants may find this a little harder than it sounds, for hitting the doll is tricky – especially after several pints.

It is very popular in Oxfordshire and the surrounding areas, where it is almost exclusively played. Most likely, it is a descendant of early bowling games, when objects were thrown rather than bowled at a target, and it is thought to have been introduced to the city of Oxford by Royalists during the Civil War, Charles I having set up court there.

However, another, somewhat less pleasant theory, is that it derives from a sport known as 'throwing at cocks', a pastime in which a cock was tied by one leg to a stake in the ground so that it could run round the stake, whereupon participants would throw 'cock-steles' (small wooden clubs) at the bird. Whoever managed to kill it, got to keep it. A later fairground amusement employed a wooden cock, where people paid to throw sticks at it.

Rules vary slightly from pub to pub, but the game may be played as follows. Each player has six sticks – not any old stick, but rather baton-shaped solid cylinders of hard or medium-density wood (Masters Traditional Games make theirs from kiln-dried beechwood), which are 18 inches (45.7 centimetres) long and 2 inches (5.1 centimetres) in diameter. Interestingly, at one time players used to oil their sticks and then bury them in sand for the winter.

Players take their throw from behind a white line or wooden strip, which is positioned about 30 feet (9.14 metres) away from the post. A throw must be underarm. The Aunt Sally doll is about 5–8 inches (12.7–20.3 centimetres) high and 3–4 inches (7.6–10.2 centimetres) wide, and should be painted white. It is actually placed on a small, round platform at one end of a horizontal 'swivel', the other end of which is stuck into the post so that it can swing freely round the post when struck.

A point is scored when a thrower unseats the doll, which is immediately put back in position for the next throw. The doll

must be dislodged without striking the post. If this occurs everyone shouts 'iron' and the throw is discounted. After six throws, the next contestant takes a turn. When all players have had their six turns, successful shots are tallied and the player with the highest score wins.

A game is usually played over several 'legs' or 'horses'. If the final result is a tie, a throw-off takes place using three sticks, and, if players are still drawn after this, the score is settled by sudden death – that is just one stick each is thrown. If a winner does not emerge at this point, the combatants throw six sticks each until, with luck, the matter is settled. However, by this time, everyone else may have returned to the bar.

Although Aunt Sally is a fun game, it is also one that regulars take very seriously, and there are a number of local leagues in Britain. Usually league play has two teams, each consisting of eight players, and three legs are played. For anyone wishing to play the game at home, the simple equipment can be purchased, although novices should take careful aim with the batons to avoid any calamities. Usually a sheet is erected behind the Aunt Sally doll to protect players and passers-by from being hit by wayward throws.

BAT AND TRAP

B AT AND TRAP is a cricket-type game played by eight
players on each side, almost exclusively in the Kent
region.

To play a grass area is chosen for the pitch, while for the
equipment one needs wooden bats with an oval face measuring not more than 8 inches (20.3 centimetres) long and
5 inches (12.7 centimetres) wide, a hard rubber ball 2 inches
(4.5 centimetres) in diameter, and a rectangular box with a
front flap – the trap. The trap is a rectangular mechanical
device which lies on the ground and propels the ball upwards
for the batsman to strike.

Two adjacent posts each measuring 7 feet (2.1 metres) are
then positioned 21 yards (19 metres) in front of the trap. A
straight white line is drawn on the ground between the posts
and a semicircular one behind them. The fielding team must
stay behind these lines, and when bowling the bowler must
keep one foot behind the line between the posts at all times.

Each player on the team has one chance to bat, with players batting until they are out. This is known as an innings.
Only one player bats at a time and once each team has played
an innings, the one with the most points wins.

To start the batsman stands beside the trap and knocks the lever down with his bat which shoots the ball upwards where it can be hit. He is allowed three attempts to hit the ball and must aim to strike the ball so it passes between the two white posts at the end of the pitch. If he misses the ball or it fails to cross the white line between the two posts or if the ball sails over the white line higher than the tops of the two white posts, he is deemed to be out.

The opposing side stand behind the white line and attempt to catch the ball. To be caught out, however, is a rare occurrence and normally a ball passes over the white line having bounced once or twice before being stopped by the fielding side.

After this part of the process is complete, the fielding side then have the chance to throw the ball back down the pitch at the trap. The fielding side's target is a black circle painted on the otherwise white trap. If they hit this target then the batsman is 'bowled out'. To increase the tension for the batsman he is allowed to do nothing to interfere with the ball as it is propelled towards the target – something not unfamiliar to certain hapless English cricketers.

If the fielding side fails to hit the target on the trap then a run is scored and the batsman lives to bat on.

Interestingly, there is a surprising amount of room left within the game for individual flair. There are no set rules for either the batting or bowling style. A batsman can hold the bat with either one or two hands, and bowlers can bowl, toss, lob or propel the ball underarm should they wish.

Bat and trap can be traced to the second millennium BC from which period relics found in a Thracian tomb near the village of Sveshtari on the Black Sea include a rudimentary trap. Flemish weavers introduced the game to Kent in the early seventeenth century, but the game dwindled and died before being re-introduced during the Great War as a form of recuperation therapy for limbless service men returning from the trenches of the Western Front.

This resurgence led to the first recorded international match between France and Britain on the eve of the advance at Passchendaele in August 1917. Alas, the outcome of that match is unknown for both teams perished on a less benign field, that of battle.

In 1921, the game re-emerged in Canterbury with the formation of the Canterbury and District Bat and Trap League. By 1951, the modern game entered a new era when floodlights were added to every league pitch allowing for later starting times. By 1982, as many as eighty teams were competing and the game had spread from Kent to Sussex and a derivative was also being played in North Yorkshire (known as 'knurl and spur') and Lincolnshire (called 'rat in the hole').

The game is now largely played in pub gardens with close to sixty pubs participating to a greater or lesser degree. Interestingly, there can never be a drawn game in bat and trap, so in theory a match could last well past the calling of last orders at the bar.

KNUR
AND SPELL

K NOWN as 'poor man's golf', the object of 'knur and spell' (a variant of 'knurl and spur') is to hit a small, hard, golf-ball sized ball – the 'knur', made of wood or earthenware – as great a distance as possible.

The 'spell' is a mechanical device similar to the trap in 'bat and trap'. When a player (also known as a 'laiker') or his caddy places a foot on the lever of the spell, the 'knur' is fired into the air, which the player then attempts to hit with a club-like stick known as a 'trippitt', 'tribbit' or 'pummel', which ranges in length from 2–6 feet (0.6–1.8 metres), and has similarities to a golf club. The shot hit the furthest distance is known as a 'cut'.

A popular game in West Yorkshire until the early twentieth century, a world-record claim was made by a Halifax 'laiker' named Fred Moore on 11 November 1889, after he hit the knur a distance of just over 372 yards (340 metres).

QUOITS

THE game of quoits involves throwing rings at a pin or stake sunk into the ground. A quoit in what is known as 'the Northern Game' is made of iron or steel, is 5–8 inches (12.7–20.3 centimetres) in diameter, and weighs around 5 lbs, while a Celtic quoit, as thrown in Wales and Scotland in what is called 'the Long Game', might weigh 10 lbs. There are even tales of quoits weighing as much as 23 lbs. Quoits are often compared in shape to the bottom of a wine glass with a hole in the middle, the top surface being referred to as 'the hill' and the concave underside as 'the hole'. In team games, when deciding who is to start play, players toss the quoit and call either 'hill' or 'hole', in the same way as head or tails is called with a coin.

Those wishing to experiment with the pastime at home may play a version known as lawn or sward quoits, which can be very enjoyable, the basic rules being simple and the equipment easy to assemble.

Place two metal pins in a designated area of lawn at a distance of 11 yards (10 metres) apart from each other. The pins must be arranged so that they stick out of the ground by 6 inches (15.2 centimetres). Each player has two quoits –

rope, rubber or plastic rings being the sensible choice for the garden game. A formal game of quoits is played with heavy rings made from iron or steel, and not only would these be dangerous to throw in the garden, but they are not suitable for children, and a casual player may find them surprisingly heavy to play with.

Each player stands alongside the near pin and throws their quoit at the far one. The basic idea is to achieve a 'ringer', that is to get one's quoit to encircle the pin. Players throw alternately and the score is added up when all quoits have been placed. A ringer scores two points, but only for the player whose quoit rings the pin last. If no one manages to get a ringer, the thrower of the quoit nearest to the pin is awarded one point. This completes an 'end', after which players collect their quoits and throw them back towards the other pin. The winner is the first to reach a score of 21 points.

Those that participate regularly often play a more tactical game. For example, although the object of the game is to ring the pin, the first player will be aware that if both he and the second player achieve a ringer, he will lose his chance of getting points. Therefore he may try for a 'cover' (where a quoit literally covers part of the top of the pin) or a 'gater' (where the quoit falls so that it rests on the pin with most of the quoit in front of it) in order to prevent the next thrower from getting his quoit to the target. Knocking other people's quoits out of the way is also considered to be fair play.

In formal games there are established names for each position in which the quoits fall. For example, if a quoit lands flat with its wider face showing, this is called 'hole-up', while a quoit that touches the side of the pin may be a 'front-toucher', 'side toucher' or a 'back toucher'. Some names are more unusual such as a 'black pot' or a 'Frenchman'.

The two most widely played games of outdoor quoits are, the Northern Game, which is played in the north of England, and the Long Game, which is played in Scotland, Wales and North Suffolk. Both are associated with pubs, where organized play really began, and are played on clay pitches, rather than grass. The clay is important as it allows the quoits to land on their edges, and there are several tactical shots that can be played in this way. The clay pitches can be messy, however. Indeed, it may be said that one of the advantages of the lawn game is that pitch maintenance is minimal.

There are marked differences between these games, the most obvious being that in the Northern Game, the quoits weigh about 5 lbs and the pins are 11 yards (10.1 metres) apart, whereas in the Long Game the quoits are much heavier and are thrown much greater distances – 18–21 yards (16.5–19.2 metres). Also, in the Northern Game, the pin rises above the clay, while in the Long Game it is set flush with the clay. Different tactics are employed in each game, with the emphasis in the Northern Game being on the scoring of ringers, and in the Long Game (where it is not really possible for more than one quoit at a time to ring the pin) on who can get closest to the target. The Long Game is often spoken of as the 'venerable' Long Game, and commands both awe and respect from those who have observed it being played. It is a game of great strength and stamina, and the ability to ring an object, that is all but invisible over such distances, seems to render spectators incredulous.

Quoits is an ancient game, but there is little concrete evidence available to us to uncover its full history. Some people are of the opinion that its roots lie in discus throwing, popular in ancient Greece, with discus throwers being much feted. However, others believe that quoits were originally weapons of war and hunting, with their weight and shape being capable of causing serious injury to foe or beast.

The Romans certainly used quoit-like objects as war weapons, and they are thought to have brought them to Britain. Possibly, the soldiers practised their throwing skills between conflicts, and the citizens of garrison towns up and down the country began to copy them.

The first official record of quoits being played in Britain is from legislation in 1361, where playing quoits was among the pursuits banned to ensure that men spent enough time at the archery butts. It was decreed that the populace were 'not to meddle in hurling of stones, loggats and coits . . . and other games of no value'. However, the public enjoyed the game, and continued to play, albeit illicitly.

In the next century, the ban on quoits was lifted, and it was so popular that taverns and alehouses often hosted games to attract customers. Consequently, the game continued to be regarded less than favourably by those in authority. Rules varied enormously. From pub to pub the size of the pitch, the weight of the quoits, the number of players, the number of targets and the number of points in a game were all open to interpretation, and this continued to be the case until the nineteenth century, when clubs devoted to the play of quoits began to be established.

In the 1880s, players in the north of England recognized the need for a more regular set of rules, and thus several clubs drew together to form the Association of Amateur Quoits Clubs for the North of England. A set of fifteen rules was arrived at which was published in *The Field* in 1881, and which have largely governed the Northern Game ever since.

Today there are several thriving leagues for the Northern Game and the National Quoits Association was formed in 1986. Meanwhile, the Long Game continues to be popular in Wales and Scotland, who play a hotly contested international match each year. However, interest in the Long Game in England has run rather low, and there has not been an international involving England since the 1960s.

*

A simpler type of garden quoits, using lightweight rope quoits that are particularly easy for children to use, can be bought from sports and garden stores in specially made up kits. The kits contain four rope quoits, a wooden-cross base, and five pegs. Four of the pegs slot into a hole at each end of the cross, and the fifth fits into the hole in the centre of the cross. The middle peg is worth 25 points, and the other four are worth 20, 15, 10 and 5 respectively.

Before the game begins, a points target must be set – perhaps a top score of 250. Each player throws his four rope quoits at the pegs, aiming to land the quoits on any of the pegs, especially the middle peg, with each throw. No points are scored for missing the pegs altogether.

The more accurate the throw the better, as the winner is the first player to reach the agreed target.

STOOLBALL

STOOLBALL has been around since at least the sixteenth century and is a forerunner of the original game of cricket. It was known to be popular in Sussex, but 'stoball' was also played in Gloucestershire and other parts of the West Country. In 1645, the Puritans saw fit to ban it, and the emerging game of cricket must also have aroused Cromwell's wrath, for he ordered the destruction of all of the cricket bats in Ireland.

Popular legend has it that milkmaids started the game by throwing stones at their upturned stools, while shepherds similarly whiled away time throwing stones at wicket (field) gates. The two became entwined and over time a cricket-type game came to be played.

Although once very popular, today stoolball is largely played as a Sussex pub garden game. Originally the stoolball was a very hard object, stuffed with quills; today a stoolball is about 7 inches (17.8 centimetres) in circumference, is solid and covered in leather, and weighs between 2 and 2.5 oz (57 and 71 grams). Bats were once described as 'staffes' and were 3 feet (0.9 metres) long. Today the game is played with rounded, wooden bats with a short handle.

To play the game, one needs first to mark out a large grass area in the middle of which is a designated strip called the 'wicket'. The boundaries of the pitch should be agreed upon before the start of play, to avoid confusion or disagreements during the game itself. If preferred, markers can be used to delineate the playing area. A 1-foot (30.5-centimetres) square board fixed to a pole, also known as the 'wicket', must be placed at either end of the strip; the wickets must face each other and there should be 16 yards (14.6 metres) between them.

The game is played – as cricket – between two teams of eleven players. Each team has one innings in which players bat and attempt to score runs while the opposing team bowls, and attempts to stop them. Eight balls bowled are called an over (unlike cricket which has six) and a set number of overs (which is agreed at the start of play) is known as an innings. An innings ends either when all the overs have been bowled or when only one batsman is left.

A coin is tossed to determine which team will bat first and which will field. The first two batsmen then position them-selves in front of the wickets and the fielders spread themselves over the pitch to maximize the chances of catching or returning the ball after the batsman strikes it. If one is short of fielders, the most essential is the wicket keeper who stands directly behind the wicket being bowled at.

When everyone is ready, the bowler bowls underarm, aim-ing to hit the wicket at the other end of the bowling crease. The batsman who is standing in front of that wicket, must ensure that the ball does not reach its target, but he must also attempt to score runs by running between the wickets.

A game of stoolball in 1878

Obviously he stands the best chance of achieving this if he hits the ball well away from the fielders.

At the end of each over, the bowler changes ends. The same person must not bowl two overs consecutively, which necessitates fielders swapping places between overs.

The advance of cricket, which was a fairly well established game in the south-east of England – particularly in the counties of Kent, Surrey and Sussex – by 1700, probably overtook stoolball, and whereas cricket went on to become a quintessentially English game, few of us have probably even heard of, let alone played stoolball. However, those keen to play a more original game in their gardens in the summer can purchase the necessary equipment for stoolball in traditional games outlets.

ACKNOWLEDGEMENTS

There are countless websites devoted to the games covered in this book, a large number of which make very interesting reading, and many of which are useful for research purposes. It is interesting to see, with regard to the history of the games included here, that in some instances the same stories are repeated verbatim, while in others there are marked differences in 'facts'. There are also many variations when describing how a game should be played. Where it was felt to be appropriate in writing this book, rules and histories were compared to official websites, but any errors in this text are the fault of the author's alone.

The following books were excellent for research purposes, and are recommended for further reading:

A Pocket Book of Marbles,
    William Bavin, Outline Press, 1991
British Sport: A Social History,
    Dennis Brailsford, The Lutterworth Press, 1992
Croquet: The Complete Guide,
    A. E. Gill, Heinemann Kingswood, 1988
Encyclopaedia Britannica
Everyday Life in Roman Britain,
    Marjorie & C. H. B. Quinnell, B. T. Batsford Limited,
    1937
Games For Court And Garden,
    Gordon Winter, The Pilot Press Limited, 1947
Kate Greenaway's Book of Games,
    Kate Greenaway, Michael O'Mara Books Limited, 1987

Mazes and Labyrinths,
   Nigel Pennick, Robert Hale Limited, 1990
Play the Game: Volleyball,
   George Bulman, Ward Lock, 1998
The Guinness Book of Cricket Facts & Feats,
   Bill Frindell, Guinness Publishing Limited, 1996
The Guinness Book of Tennis Facts & Feats,
   Lance Tingay, Guinness Superlatives Limited, 1983
The Handbook of Cricket,
   Keith Andrew, Pelham Books, 1989
The New BBC Book of Bowls,
   Keith Phillips, BBC Consumer Publishing, 1990
The Pernod Book of Pétanque,
   Maurice Abney-Hastings, George Allen & Unwin
   Limited, 1981
Tennis, Squash and Badminton Bygones,
   Gerald N. Gurney, Shire Publications Limited, 1984